How to Sue Your Lawyer:

**THE CONSUMER
GUIDE TO
LEGAL MALPRACTICE**

HILTON L. STEIN

LEGAL MALPRACTICE INSTITUTE
103 Washington Street, Department 158
Morristown, New Jersey 07960
(201) 267-1161

#19963872

0-92

How to Sue Your Lawyer:
THE CONSUMER
GUIDE TO
LEGAL MALPRACTICE
by
HILTON L. STEIN

Published by:
LEGAL MALPRACTICE INSTITUTE
103 Washington Street
Department 158
Morristown, New Jersey 07960
(201) 267-1161
HILTON L. STEIN

This book is designed to provide accurate and authoritative information in regard to the subjects covered. The publisher is not, however, engaged in rendering legal services. If legal advice or other professional assistance is required, the services of a competent professional should be sought.

LIBRARY OF CONGRESS
CATALOGING-IN-PUBLICATION DATA

Stein, Hilton L, 1946-
    How to sue your lawyer.
        1. Lawyers—Malpractice—United States—
        Popular works. I. Title.
KF313.Z9S74 1989   346.7303'3   89-2636
ISBN 0-945163-01-0   347.30633

Design & Typography by TeleSet, Inc., Somerville, NJ

I dedicate this book to:

The memory of my parents, Sid and Shirley Stein, who created the foundation of life in me of strength, character, and compassion.

To Sito and Jido Ajjan, my in-laws, who have always been by my side and made this project possible.

To my children: Seth, whose brightness is the shining star in my life; Stephanie, whose charm always warms my heart; Marc, my lovable clone; and Lauren, whose birth is God's gift. May our paths of life always parallel one another.

To my wife, Karen, we have finally made it!!!

I acknowledge:

the assistance in the completion of this book of my typists Judy Koldyk and Julia Orriss, and of the editors of this book for their editorial assistance, John Rogalski and Jane Schlesser. Isabel S. Grossner was responsible for the final editing and proofreading of the completed manuscript. I also want to thank Rolf E. Hiebler, Esq. for his contribution.

I must also thank Stephen "Skip" Weinstein, Esq. for his steadfast loyalty and friendship.

Contents

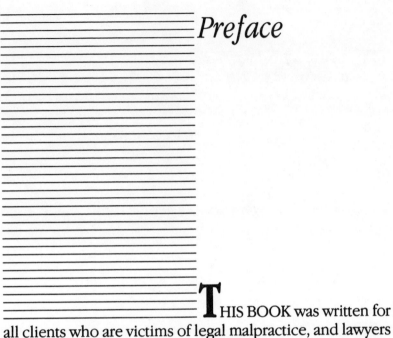# *Preface*

THIS BOOK was written for all clients who are victims of legal malpractice, and lawyers suing other lawyers for legal malpractice. For the non-lawyer client, this book helps determine whether a lawyer has mishandled the case and, if so, how to assert a claim for legal malpractice. For the lawyer suing another lawyer for legal malpractice, the book provides a step-by-step guide to the claim and the lawsuit process. For both clients and lawyers it provides creative solutions to the problems associated with legal malpractice.

The magnitude of the current legal malpractice crisis is reflected in staggering statistics: both the severity and the frequency of legal malpractice claims are increasing rapidly. There is a conspiracy of silence by lawyers concerning lawyer negligence. Lawyers, moreover, cover up their mistakes. This crisis is here to stay. This guide, therefore, is my personal attempt through information, details, forms, and suggested solutions to provide both the lawyer as well as the non-lawyer client with insight into the many aspects of legal malpractice.

My own experience has given me a unique insight into the mystique surrounding lawyers' professional liability insurance and legal malpractice claims. After ten years in the private practice of law, including making legal malpractice claims against attorneys, I developed a modestly successful suburban law practice. After a series of problems, professional and personal, I withdrew from the practice of law. My conduct came under review and ultimately I was disciplined by the New Jersey Supreme Court. In 1984 the Court imposed a six-month suspension on my privilege to practice law. While this was happening, I joined a malpractice insurance carrier, beginning as a claims examiner in the lawyers and accountants professional malpractice unit. There I applied the experience and skills I had developed as a practicing attorney handling professional liability claims. In 1983 I was promoted to supervisor of the unit. Later in 1983 I was selected to create and manage a nationwide professional liability claims department. Shortly thereafter, in 1984, I opened my own consulting and insurance adjusting firm. This firm serviced insurance carriers, professional associations, and managing general agents, in both the United States and Canada. Since then I have performed studies and lectured about professional liability claims handling and suing lawyers for legal malpractice.

When I re-entered the practice of law in 1986, I primarily defended professionals, mostly lawyers, against claims of legal malpractice and also represented insurance carriers in cases where professional liability insurance coverage was an issue.

In 1988 I left the defense practice to concentrate my efforts on establishing a law practice focused on suing lawyers. I was discovered by David Sittenfeld, one of the producers of "The Morton Downey Jr. Show." After several appearances on television, my practice boomed. It is from this base of experience that I created the Legal Malpractice Institute to provide creative solutions to the legal malpractice crisis. The result of that effort is *How to Sue Your Lawyer: The Consumer Guide to Legal Malpractice.* ≡

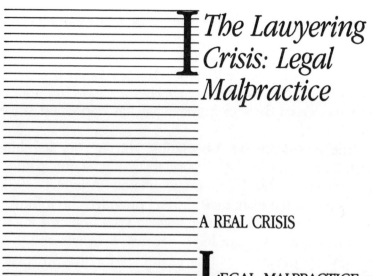

I The Lawyering Crisis: Legal Malpractice

A REAL CRISIS

LEGAL MALPRACTICE was once a little known phenomenon in American jurisprudence, but it has now reached crisis proportions. Claims of legal malpractice are increasing at an alarming rate. Attorney malpractice is no longer a problem for just the legal community. It now affects all of us. In fact, the way our society deals with this crisis should be a national concern. Instead, the response to date borders on a national scandal.

There is a conspiracy of silence by lawyers concerning legal malpractice. Lawyers cover up their mistakes. Lawyers will deny that any mistakes were ever made. The media pay too little attention to it. The crisis is real. The client, therefore, must unravel the mystery of legal malpractice. *How to Sue Your Lawyer: The Consumer Guide to Legal Malpractice* is the first step.

AN OVERVIEW

I PREDICT that, in 1989, one out of every ten lawyers will be sued for legal malpractice. This is only the beginning of the explosion of legal malpractice lawsuits. In 1985 one out of every seventeen lawyers practicing in the United States was visited

1

with a claim of legal malpractice. In the same year, in some parts of the country, such as Los Angeles County, a claim was made against one in every six lawyers. To better understand this crisis, let's examine what has happened since 1980.

The American Bar Association, through its Standing Committee of Lawyers' Professional Liability, started gathering statistics on legal malpractice claims in January 1981. Legal malpractice insurance carriers provided the information to the National Legal Malpractice Data Center. I know how this study was completed because I participated in it through my job as a claims examiner for the American International Group. As we opened each claim file we completed a report that was ultimately sent to the Data Center, where the information was computerized. The Center made an analysis of 29,227 legal malpractice claims reported from January 1983 through September 30, 1985. Ultimately, the *Profile of Legal Malpractice: A Statistical Study of Determinative Characteristics of Claims Asserted against Attorneys* was published in 1986. The results were shocking. Forty-four percent of the claims made against lawyers were the result of what were called "substantive errors." These errors included: failure to know or properly apply the law, 10 percent of all claims; inadequate discovery of facts or investigation of claims, 9 percent of all claims: planning error in choice of procedures, 8 percent of all claims; and failure to know or ascertain deadlines, 7 percent of all claims. Twenty-six percent of all claims were described as "administrative errors." This category included: failure to calendar properly, 11 percent of all claims; procrastination or lack of follow-up, 5 percent of all claims; and failure to file documents where no deadline was involved, 4 percent of all claims.

"Client relations errors" accounted for 16 percent of all legal malpractice claims. This category included: failure to obtain a client's consent or to inform a client, 9 percent of all claims; and failure to follow client's instructions, 6 percent of all claims.

The last major category was "intentional wrongs," which represented 12 percent of the total claims made.

Specific areas of legal malpractice where errors are continuously made and examples of those errors can be found in Chapter III. Even in the few years since this study ended, malpractice claims have increased dramatically. With the ranks of attorneys swelling, the number of incidents of legal malpractice will soar in even greater proportions. There are now close to seven hundred thousand practicing attorneys in the United States. It will not be long before there are a million. Imagine the crisis we are now experiencing increasing with this influx of new attorneys! The predictable results will overwhelm our present system of insurance, claims, and lawsuits. The consumer will be the victim.

THE IMPACT OF THE CRISIS

ONE ONLY needs to look at the work lawyers have traditionally done for clients to gauge the impact of legal malpractice. Lawyers have been friends, business associates, and financial advisors. The lawyer acts as a personal counselor to a client as well as a source of information and guidance about the law. The client increasingly becomes dependent on the attorney. When the attorney errs or acts negligently, the client suffers. The statistics show how widespread legal malpractice has become and the numbers of clients who have suffered. As more attorneys commit malpractice, the impact of this crisis will only grow.

What is the remedy for a client hurt by an attorney's malpractice? A lawsuit with (presumably) a malpractice insurance carrier paying the ultimate adverse judgement, award, or settlement seems to be the only answer. Thus, there is no question that legal malpractice insurance will become increasingly difficult to obtain as the losses experienced by insurers increase. Ultimately it will be the clients, the final consumers of legal services, who will pay for the increased cost of lawyers' malpractice insurance. Unfortunately, more and more law firms will find that they are simply uninsurable as a result of claims made against them. In some jurisdictions more than one-third of the practicing bar is now uninsured. What does this mean to lawyers and clients? Our primary concern should be the fair and adequate compensation of victims of legal malpractice. In trying to accommodate the client's interests, we encounter the real problem: How is a legal malpractice suit resolved fairly? Regrettably, the entire process of legal malpractice claims has remained a mystery for too long. It is now time for answers to this problem of legal malpractice, its process, and its implications.

It is universally accepted that the worst fate that could befall any client is to have to retain one lawyer to sue another lawyer when the client was right in the first place.

It is difficult for clients to hire lawyers and deal with the system. The legal process is a frustrating one for any person. Once the lawyer is guilty of legal malpractice, the client must now hire a second lawyer to sue the first lawyer. This is even more difficult because, as the victim will soon discover, hiring the second lawyer to sue the first lawyer is more difficult than hiring the first lawyer. There are not many lawyers willing to sue other lawyers. This crisis leaves a segment of our society disenfranchised by the system.

I have found thousands of people who are victims of legal malpractice in this country, unable to find lawyers who are willing to sue lawyers who are guilty of legal malpractice. Many lawyers claim they don't want to sue other lawyers. When lawyers are willing to sue other lawyers, the cases they are willing to handle are limited to those situations where both gross malpractice on the part of the lawyer and a substantial dollar recovery are involved. Unless these two factors are present, the consumer of legal services will have a difficult time finding a lawyer willing to sue another lawyer.

My own experience illustrates how an attorney out of control impacts on society. ≡

# II Out of Control

WHILE ATTENDING law school at the University of Akron School of Law, I was recognized for my achievements. I served on the prestigious *Akron Law Review* as a staff member during all three years of law school. I was also editor-in-chief of the *Arete*, the law school journal.

I was a bright young lawyer who completed law school with high expectations, and I wanted to achieve excellence in the profession. I wanted to have an impact on society through my work. Of course, I also hoped for economic success, but this was a secondary desire. Thus, as most serious young attorneys do, I applied myself, working diligently, and anticipated early success.

After graduation from law school, I had the privilege of serving a clerkship with one of the finest judges in New Jersey. I was able to participate in the judicial decision-making process, the most rewarding experience of my young legal career. I learned the law from a practical perspective. My mentor to this day stands out as one of the most distinguished judges to ever sit on the bench. After the end of my clerkship, I worked for several law firms, eventually establishing my own practice in suburban Morris County, New Jersey.

By this time I was married, had two children, and owned my own house in the suburbs, and had presumably

6

achieved the American dream. Regrettably, it was the very pursuit of this dream that ultimately became a nightmare for me. In fact, CBS News later referred to this time of my life as being "out of control." My circumstances and experiences during this period were extreme, but it is important to remember that statistics indicate other lawyers will encounter at least one of the problems I faced during this time.

I had achieved recognition as a leading trial attorney. As a consequence, I was appointed municipal prosecutor for a number of townships. My reputation grew in the area where I practiced, and I decided to add several members to my law firm. With the growth of my practice, job-related stress increased enormously and my failing marriage compounded these pressures. During this stressful time I failed to take proper care of my health and so I suffered a series of weakening maladies. My physicians responded to my ailments by prescribing all sorts of drugs, and I became dependent on some of them. It became easy for me to rely upon nonprescriptive drugs to get me through my average eighteen-hour workdays.

My marriage deteriorated even further. Without realizing it, I was letting my practice slowly slip away. My personal and professional life continued to worsen. Eventually I realized it was necessary for me to get my life back under control and, to do so, I decided that I had to withdraw from one of my life's loves: the practice of law.

Attorneys are trained to practice law. We know no other way to make a living. As a result of my withdrawal from practice, I was left without a livelihood. My situation was further worsened when the Ethics Committee began proceedings against me, threatening to take away my license to practice law. The attorney with whom I had practiced started a lawsuit against me. All at once many administrative hearings began, and by that time I did not have the strength or finances to defend myself. As a trial attorney I had performed substantial *pro bono* work, but none of that seemed to matter. I was ready to surrender my license.

Although my inclination was to give up my license to practice law, a lawyer by the name of Stephen "Skip" Weinstein, who came to my assistance as a friend, would not let me. Skip attended countless hearings with me, and worked in the evenings, on weekends, and holidays. Ultimately the Supreme Court of New Jersey heard my case and imposed a six-month suspension on my privilege to practice law.

In the meantime, I started a vigorous exercise program and my health gradually improved. I had a renewed commitment to return to my profession. I refused to accept defeat, and committed myself to establishing a stronger, revitalized standard of excellence for myself and the legal profession. I decided I would help lawyers having problems overcome the obstacles I faced.

CAUSES & CONSEQUENCES

ONE OUT of every six lawyers may be impaired. The cause of these impairments may be simply a result of stress from managing a law practice. Or it may be the stress placed on an attorney in a large firm who aspires to be a partner. Once achieving that goal, the attorney is then confronted with attaining his or her quota of billable hours and clients. The pressures increase. The attorney in a small or medium-size practice faces the same pressures. Since stress is caused by a variety of pressures and situations, its results are also varied. Stress often causes illness, incapacitation, and even disease. Thus it is not surprising that enormous job stresses result in attorneys being impaired. Those impairments will undoubtedly affect the practice itself. There is no attorney that can practice law while fighting a bitterly contested matrimonial or custody proceeding without suffering an adverse impact on his or her own practice. No attorney confronted with serious health problems can withstand the stress of a demanding law practice. Alcohol and drug abuse, common among practicing lawyers, will also prevent an attorney from attaining a high level of competence and responsiveness to clients. It's important to realize that since no lawyer is exempt from stress and impairment, no lawyer is exempt from being sued for malpractice.

BAPTISM BY FIRE

THE ASSOCIATION of Trial Lawyers of America, in reviewing my professional experiences, called my expertise in professional liability claims handling a "baptism by fire." There is no better way to describe my experience. After withdrawing from the practice of law, I pounded the pavement looking for work. I finally saw a classified ad seeking adjusters or examiners to handle lawyers' professional liability claims. I was convinced that my own experience made me uniquely qualified for that job. I vigorously pursued it, and after an exhaustive effort, I was hired. Unfortunately, my salary didn't even approach the amount of alimony and child support I was responsible for paying to my ex-wife, but at least it was a beginning of a new career.

My job required that I receive, review, and analyze first notice claims against attorneys and accountants accused of malpractice or negligence. I was to review the claim and determine which aspects would be covered under the insurance policy. I would then assign counsel for either the defense of the matter or for a declaratory action to determine whether there was insurance coverage. I also issued disclaimer letters and reservation-of-rights letters to insureds, to tell them whether or not all or part of a particular complaint would be covered by their insurance policies. I was to monitor the lawyers I assigned and settle claims. I would also make recommendations to my supervisors about settlement of high exposure claims.

As a practicing attorney I handled claims against professionals, including claims against attorneys, yet I knew almost nothing about the internal workings of an insurance company. Nor did I understand anything about the mystique surrounding lawyers' professional liability claims. During my time in this job, I had firsthand experience in dealing directly with claimants who had filed complaints or claims against lawyers. These people were the victims of legal malpractice. I dealt directly with the insured attorneys who were defendants. I also coordinated the various lawyers: defense counsel, personal counsel, and coverage counsel. In short, I handled all aspects of lawyers' professional liability claims.

After a year as a claims examiner and adjuster, I was promoted to supervisor of claims of the lawyers' and accountants' malpractice unit. In this position I had the opportunity to supervise one-half of all claims made against the many attorneys insured by the largest malpractice insurance carrier in the world. I was also responsible for the review and supervision of half the professional liability claims examiners or adjusters in the company. Soon after, I was selected to implement a nationwide professional liability claims department.

As manager of the professional liability claims department, I was responsible for the transfer of thousands of claims from local adjustment offices into three regional offices. I assisted in hiring and training claims people nationwide. I also served as liaison to managing general agents of professional associations. I had the responsibility of examining every claim that was filed in excess of a hundred thousand dollars of exposure for recovery by claimants. I served the underwriting department by reviewing insurance policies governing professional associations. For example, I visited those associations and lectured about professional liability claims. I assisted in renewing those professional liability programs and renegotiating various insurance policies. I had the unique opportunity to travel throughout the United States and talk to claimants, attorneys, insurance people, and all others involved with professional liability.

The crisis was obvious to me. Underlying this crisis, there existed a basic misunderstanding of the way professional liability claims were handled. Since the insurance industry was not about to change its practices, I realized that this crisis affected our entire society. I watched firsthand as claimants, attorneys, and insureds all suffered as a result of the complex legal malpractice system. A spokesperson was needed to address these issues.

RE-ENTERING THE PRACTICE OF LAW

ONCE MY license was restored, I returned to the practice of law, where I could have an impact on lawyers' malpractice. I reopened a law office just yards away from my last one. I knew that my main objective was to improve the treatment of lawyers' professional liability claims. Soon after opening my practice, I joined a firm that defended professional liability claims. We represented professionals, mainly lawyers, who had been charged with malpractice. I also represented insurance companies in providing coverage opinions arising out of professional liability disputes with the insureds.

Here I again saw the crisis in professional liability claims. Premiums were soaring. Insureds were dissatisfied with the complex system for handling claims. Claimants, the victims of legal malpractice, cried out for justice. The system simply moved too slowly to provide the justice the parties so desperately needed. I decided once again to attempt to find a forum for debate of these problems.

I wrote an article to alert lawyers about the right way to respond to a claim of legal malpractice. This article was featured by the *New Jersey Law Journal* and made me visible in the state bar structure. I received calls about how lawyers should handle a malpractice claim. What I saw was lawyers simply ignoring claims of legal malpractice or, worse, covering them up.

A local news network then carried a feature story about legal malpractice. I thought I finally had the appropriate forum. The network visited me, intending to use my experience as a featured presentation: I was recommended by the state-sponsored legal malpractice carrier as the individual who would have expertise in this area. During my discussion with the media people, I told them that I had been disciplined by the New Jersey Supreme Court, and agreed to discuss the facts and circumstances surrounding those unpleasant years.

The news team came to my office and spent an hour and a half taping interviews with me about legal malpractice. When the news carried this story, the station devoted one-and-one-half minutes to my unfortunate experience. Regrettably, that seemed to be the only segment shown on TV. In addition to a change in my story's focus, there were misstatements about my background, dramatizing my area of vulnerability. I knew then that my goal had not been achieved and that I would have to take more aggressive action to create nationwide interest in lawyers' professional liability. I left the defense practice. I opened a law office devoted to suing lawyers. I also created the Legal Malpractice Institute.

LEGAL MALPRACTICE INSTITUTE

WHILE PRACTICING law, I was actively involved in both the local and state bar committees governing impaired lawyers. Specifically, I joined the State Bar Association Special Committee on Drug and Alcohol Abuse. The local Morris County Bar Association also established a Lawyers' Assistance Committee. In this committee I was responsible for devising a plan to help lawyers who were suffering from drug or alcohol abuse, stress, or physical illnesses.

The creation of the Legal Malpractice Institute was designed to implement creative solutions to the problems surrounding lawyers' malpractice. I also wanted to assist victims of legal malpractice. The Legal Malpractice Institute's first goal was to publish the book I intended to write about legal malpractice, in an effort to gain nationwide attention to the problem. When *Trial* magazine adapted my article and gave me national exposure, I knew that the Legal Malpractice Institute would be the mechanism through which I would be able to spread my knowledge of legal malpractice problems.

Ultimately, the Legal Malpractice Institute will offer seminars, programs, and practical advice from the claims perspective to all persons involved in legal malpractice. The Legal Malpractice Institute is now drafting a plan for referral lists of attorneys who are willing to sue other attorneys. It will also monitor lawyers on behalf of corporate America to reduce what can only be described as runaway legal fees and unaccounted for legal malpractice at the highest levels. The Institute will also serve as a consumer-oriented entity by providing seminars and lectures to consumer groups to educate individual clients on how to identify legal malpractices and pursue whatever remedies may be appropriate.

DAVID SITTENFELD
& "THE MORTON DOWNEY JR. SHOW"

SOON AFTER the television news debacle, I called several television stations in an effort to publicize the crisis in legal malpractice. One of the producers I spoke with was David Sittenfeld, producer of "The Morton Downey Jr. Show." I explained to him why I had left the defense practice and was now devoting all new cases to only suing lawyers. He wondered how a client was able to sue a lawyer for legal malpractice. I explained to him how the entire process worked. He then asked me, if he should hire a lawyer and that lawyer were negligent, he could then hire another lawyer to sue the first lawyer? I informed him that was precisely what my practice was all about. I advised him I intended to write a book which was in its final stages concerning the rights of clients in suing lawyers for legal malpractice. I was instructed to send all the material concerning what I was doing in this area of legal malpractice directly to David Sittenfeld's attention: I did so.

David Sittenfeld, as soon as he received my materials, immediately followed up by directing other members of the production staff to interview me for an appearance on "The Morton Downey Jr. Show." At that time the Downey Show was a local, New York metropolitan, television program. Soon after my first taped appearance, in which I challenged another lawyer concerning the issue of legal malpractice, the Downey Show went into national syndication. I thereafter became a regular guest on the show and assisted in the production of many segments. I was also asked to accompany Morton Downey, Jr., for live appearances on his stage shows, and later served as his legal consultant.

In the interim, my law practice boomed. I had people that were desperate, calling me from all over the country seeking the advice of a lawyer who was willing to sue other lawyers for legal malpractice. I couldn't even handle the volume of calls which were coming into an "800" number which I had established. The number of calls was overwhelming. I had became a national celebrity for suing lawyers. The consumer was now ready for a change. ≡

III Legal Malpractice: Let's Look at It

DEFINITION

LEGAL MALPRACTICE has already been referred to as a recent phenomenon in American law. In fact, *Black's Law Dictionary* defined the term "malpractice" in 1968 as "occasionally applied to lawyers, and then means generally any evil practice in a professional capacity, but rather with reference to the court and its practice and process rather than to the client" (4th edition, West Publishing Co.). The concept of an attorney being held liable for acts of professional negligence is still in its early stages of development. As a consequence, authorities often differ about the definition of legal malpractice. The majority of experts, however, define the phrase in terms of a standard of care and a deviation from that standard. A later edition of *Black's,* in 1979, defined "legal malpractice" as the "failure of an attorney to use such skill, prudence and possess and exercise in performance of tasks which they undertake, and when such failure proximately causes damages it gives rise to an action in tort." (revised 4th edition, West Publishing Co.). Cases, throughout the United States, generally hold that legal malpractice may be defined as the failure of an attorney to use and exercise such skill, prudence, and diligence as other members of the legal profession commonly possess and exercise in representing clients. These definitions are, of course, broad standards employed in determining whether a lawyer has deviated from the ordinary standard of performance by attorneys. Other authorities use standards relating the lawyer's possession and exercise of knowledge and skill to specific situations. Another variation of a definition involves the application of that knowledge to specific kinds of cases.

The authorities almost always define legal malpractice in a traditional tort sense, and attach traditional negligence theories to legal malpractice. Thus, a plaintiff suing an attorney for legal malpractice will generally have to rely upon traditional negligence doctrines in pursuing the claim. Therefore, such a plaintiff must establish three things: duty, breach of that duty, and proximate cause between the breach and the actual damage that resulted.

It appears that an action for legal malpractice is a hybrid cause of action in that there are elements that involve other theories of liability, including breach of implied and express warranties. It has also been suggested that an attorney's undertaking to represent a client is contractual in nature and, therefore, any breach by an attorney may result in distinct cause of action in contract.

There are a number of reasons why a plaintiff suing an attorney for malpractice would want to pursue causes of action other than those based on negligence. Procedural and substantive grounds may expand the scope of a plaintiff's cause of action against an attorney. On the other hand, a plaintiff might want to rely upon a negligence theory, particularly when the plaintiff is not a client of the attorney. Under certain circumstances the non-client may be better served by pursuing an action based on a negligence theory.

I disapprove of the authorities that look to any one of these theories as a strict, conclusive guide to determine whether an attorney is guilty of malpractice. These definitions are created by lawyers for lawyers. Rather, I view legal malpractice in a subjective sense and I am more comfortable with defining it in a very basic way, unrelated to the

traditional notions of tort or contract law. Thus, legal malpractice should be determined according to whether or not
there is an act, error or omission by an attorney in rendering
or failing to render professional services which results in
damages or harm. Most legal malpractice insurance policies
contain coverage language similar to these terms. Tort liability requires proximate cause. In my judgment, whether
or not the damage is proximately caused by attorney malpractice should not be a factor in deciding whether a claim
should be brought. In other words, an attorney may be
guilty of legal malpractice, but the legal malpractice may
not result in economic loss. The result of legal malpractice
may be the loss of opportunity. Let's examine this concept
of proximate cause in a theoretical sense, and then make a
practical application.

A victim of legal malpractice who wants to sue the
lawyer must establish a connection between the negligence
of the lawyer and the damage suffered by the client. This
connection is called proximate cause (Prosser, *Law of Torts,*
4th edition, West Publishing Co., 1971, p. 236). In an eso-
teric sense, "causation is a fragile thread which connects
the concept of fault to the reality of damage" (Mallen and
Levit, *Legal Malpractice,* 2nd edition, West Publishing Co.,
1981, p. 177). This means that the attorney is only liable
for those damages proximately caused by the attorney's
conduct. The widely accepted view is that an attorney will
not be liable for committing an act, error, or omission
unless it satisfies the traditional notions of negligence law
which requires proof of proximate cause. Let's use a basic
example of attorney malpractice to demonstrate the
dilemma involved in making definitions. Assume that Mr.
Malpractice is retained to defend a client who has been
sued for breach of contract. Mr. Malpractice fails to appear at
the calendar call and a default is entered against the client.
The client decides to sue the attorney for legal malpractice
before the plaintiff tries to collect judgment against the

client. In the traditional negligence sense, the client has not yet suffered any damages from the attorney's malpractice. Until the plaintiff attempts execution of the judgment against the client, the claim of legal malpractice is not yet matured.

The client is unable to prove any damages proximately caused by the negligence of the lawyer. Moreover, the client must prove that he or she would have won the underlying case before the client can recover in the malpractice action against the lawyer. This is commonly referred to as the "but for" test. Mr. Malpractice would argue in his defense that the client would have had to pay the damages after losing the underlying trial even if default had not been entered. The lawyer would argue, therefore, that the client should have paid the plaintiff in the first place. In other words, the plaintiff would have won the case even if the lawyer was not negligent.

In the majority of jurisdictions, traditional definitions hinder a client from pursuing a cause of action in legal malpractice. In contrast, using my definition (legal malpractice as defined as an act, error, or omission by an attorney in rendering or failing to render professional services which result in damages or harm), the attorney indeed committed malpractice and has damaged the client. Taken one step further, the mere fact that the client was deprived of the opportunity to litigate the case and defend himself or herself would automatically be considered damages or harm, giving rise to a legal malpractice action. See *Lieberman v. Employers Insurance of Wausau,* 84 N.J. 325 (1980); *Lamb v. Barbour,* 188 N.J. Super 6 (App. Div. 1982), Cert. denied, 93 N.J. 297 (1983); *Mant v. Gillespie,* 189 N.J. Super 368 (App. Div. 1983); *Allied Productions, Inc. v. Duesterdick,* 232 So. E. 2nd 744 (Va. 1977).

Another theory advanced in legal malpractice has been referred to as the "case within a case" theory or as the "trial within a trial" theory. In its basic form, the trial of a legal malpractice case would necessarily involve a trial of the underlying action. Let's say Mr. Malpractice allows a default to be entered against his client and then is sued by the client for legal malpractice. During the course of the trial against Mr. Malpractice, the proceedings would necessarily involve a conclusion about, or at least production of all of the evidence that would have been heard, in the underlying case against the client. This theory is explored later in this text, but it is mentioned here because of its impact. Some courts have disapproved a strict case within a case theory. If one were to adopt my definition of legal malpractice as an act, error or omission in rendering or failing to render professional services for others, which results in damage or harm to a client, there would be no need for the trial within a trial method. Rather, the fact finder or jury would be entitled to assess damages for economic injuries or harm arising out of the attorney's failure to properly defend the underlying case.

There is also an entire body of law that defines legal malpractice by what it is not. It is universally accepted that an attorney is not an insurer of his results. Nor does he guarantee his work product. Generally, errors in judgment have been held not actionable under the traditional theory. See *Leighton v. New York Susquehanna and Western Railroad*, 303 F. Supp. 599, 618 (Southern District, N.Y. 1969); *McCullough v. Sullivan*, 102 N.J.L. 383, 384 (E & A 1926).

I served the insurance industry in the area of lawyers' malpractice as a consultant in a variety of capacities. One matter in which I was retained involved a landmark decision which was reported in New Jersey as *Procanik v. Cillo*, 206 N.J. Super. 270 (Law Div. 1986); reversed, 226 N.J. Super. 132 (App. Div. 1988); Petition for Certification denied, 113 N.J. 357 (1988). In that case the Trial Court wrote an opinion which set up different standards of care for a specialist in the practice of law as compared to a general practitioner. The Trial Court was overruled by the

Appellate Division. The Supreme Court refused to take certification of the case. Thus, the original decision was overturned and a judgment was entered in favor of the defendant-lawyers. The distinction between generalists and specialists in the practice of law in the context of legal malpractice is not clear. For example, is the law practitioner who engages in only one aspect of law deemed to be a specialist? Most jurisdictions will not allow an attorney to advertise a specialty in a particular discipline. Yet an attorney who has tried a number of civil or criminal cases may, under certain circumstances, be tested and certified as a trial attorney without any substantive expertise in any particular subject area of the law. The issue of whether an attorney who engages primarily in one aspect of substantive law may be a specialist for the purposes of legal malpractice is not well settled. The *Procanik* case illustrates the early stages of what I predict will be considerable litigation to settle this issue. In *Procanik,* the trial judge determined that the specialist had a duty to disclose to his client what was described as a complete opinion, giving full informed judgment that a settled law is ripe for reconsideration. In the absence of this complete disclosure, a jury could find that an attorney-client relationship has not ended, and in accordance with the trial judge's opinion in *Procanik,* there would be a continuing obligation to inform the client as to any changes in the law. In other words the attorney-client relationship would continue beyond the apparent termination. As mentioned, that decision was subsequently overturned when the Appellate Division ruled in favor of the defendant-lawyers as a matter of law. The Supreme Court of New Jersey would not review the Appellate Division.

Recently, other courts have allowed causes of action for legal malpractice when one attorney misrepresents to another attorney his intention to proceed at a calendar call (*Malewich v. Zacharias,* 196 N.J. Super 372 [App. Div. 1984]).

There may be a duty from one attorney to another to make open and full disclosure, even in an adversarial situation. In other words, breach of ethical responsibilities between one attorney and another may give rise to a separate cause of action. In other jurisdictions, courts have allowed various causes of action, like abuse of process or malicious prosecution. Rule 11 of the *Federal Rules of Civil Procedure* allow sanctions to be imposed against attorneys for vexatious litigation.

In all of these situations, the conduct of the attorney may be defined as constituting legal malpractice if my definition, instead of the traditional definition, is applied. The distinction lies in a practical versus a theoretical approach to defining legal malpractice.

Let's be concerned with the rights of the consumer of legal services. Expand the definition of legal malpractice to allow access for victims of legal malpractice!

LEGAL MALPRACTICE: HERE IT IS

THE PROFILE of Legal Malpractice: A Statistical Study of Determinative Characteristics of Claims Asserted against Attorneys, a 1986 report by the Standing Committee on Lawyer's Professional Liability of the American Bar Association, was based on approximately thirty thousand claims made against attorneys. These claims were reported to the National Legal Malpractice Data Center from January 1983 through September 30, 1985. The study provides an excellent base for analyzing the nature of claims made against insured attorneys. Understanding the method through which this study was conducted is essential; thus, an explanation of the process through which the information was gathered is necessary.

Each participating insurance company instructed its legal malpractice claims examiners and adjusters to fill out a "National Legal Malpractice Data Center Reporting Form" for each claim. This form separated data into four categories. The first claims examiner was charged with completing each of the four sections. The first section, further divided into fifteen subcategories, asked the status of the claim, where the claim was made, and the number of lawyers insured under the complained-against lawyer's insurance policy. Questions in this section also concerned the number of years the insured had been an attorney when the alleged error was made, what kind of practice the insured had (whether it was a legal clinic, legal aid, or private practice), the relationship of the insured to the claimant, and whether or not the insured's effort to collect a fee gave rise to the claim. There were also questions about whether or not the claim came from an area normally within the attorney's practice. The form required specific data about the date of the occurrence and the date it was reported. This first section also contained information about closed claims. In these cases, the claims examiner was to show whether or not the claim was abandoned; suit was commenced; judgment was paid, and if it was, the amount, and the expenses involved, including the deductible paid by the insured attorney.

The second section of the form questioned the area of law involved. This subdivision contained twenty-five categories, ranging from trust and probate to natural resources. The third major section defined the specific kind of legal activity that led to the claim, like the start of a legal action, pre-trial or pre-hearing trial, post-trial, and so on. Another question asked about other activities, which couldn't be categorized in the fifteen regular subsections. The last section indicated "the most significant to the cause of the claim being made." This section listed twenty-two separate categories, like failure to calendar properly, failure to react to a calendar date, failure to know or learn a deadline correctly, clerical error, and planning or strategy error.

As in the previous section, the examiner was free to indicate a cause that did not appear on the list.

The Data Center gathered detailed information about most claims filed during its existence. Experience teaches that the claims, with few exceptions, have not changed dramatically since the study and therefore remains the best, and in fact, the only significant national source of statistical information on malpractice claims against attorneys. To fully grasp the intensity of the crisis in legal malpractice, it is necessary to examine in detail *The Profile of Legal Malpractice*.

First, let's examine the areas of law where claims are being made against attorneys. An interesting observation reported in the *Profile* is that 84 percent of claims arose out of eight areas of the law. Therefore, only 16 percent of claims came from the other seventeen areas. The eight areas: Personal Injury-Property Damage, Plaintiff, 25 percent; Real Estate, 23 percent; Collection and Bankruptcy, 10 percent; Family Law, 8 percent; Estate Trust and Probate, 7 percent; Corporate and Business Organization, 5 percent; Criminal, 3 percent; Personal Injury-Property Damage, Defendant, 3 percent.

The study points out, however, that "some areas may include other specific transactions." It cites as an example a business or commercial activity that may involve a real estate transaction. I would rather consider this area mere overlap. From my own experience, I have found that many data sheets were completed at the first notice. Therefore, there was some unreliability in these forms. Many first notice claims arose out of law suits. These claims would usually come into the office with merely a complaint and summons attached. In most of these cases very little information was available for a precise statement of the nature and extent of the claim. The examiner was, however, generally able to determine the area of the law. If the claims examiner or adjuster was uncertain, he would make an educated guess, which usually proved to be accurate.

In the category describing the activity in which the attorney was engaged at the time the error occurred, there were fifteen subcategories from which the examiner could choose. Six of these categories were described as "litigation activities." They accounted for 53 percent of all claims. Litigation activities include: starting an action, pre-trial or pre-hearing proceedings, trial or hearing, post-trial or hearing, appeal, settlement and negotiation. The relationship described by the *Profile* shows that commencing an action represented 47 percent of the malpractice litigation claims; pretrial, 15 percent; trial, 13 percent; post-trial, 5 percent; appeal, 5 percent; and settlement, 15 percent. The *Profile* concluded that litigation seems to produce a lower risk of substantive errors, but administrative errors are more likely. This is further evidenced by the conclusion that 21 percent of all claims arose from the preparation of documents; 11 percent from consultation or advice; and 5 percent from title opinions. All other activities represented only 10 percent of all claims. Further analysis reveals that personal injury, which represented 25 percent of all claims, accounted for 42 percent of all litigation activities. Real estate, by contrast, represented a substantially smaller percentage of litigation activity, 12 percent. Criminal defense practice and the defendant's personal injury-property damage practice, while each represented 3 percent of all claims, each accounted for 5 percent of all litigation activity.

Of all claims involving plaintiff's personal injury and property damage practice, 50 percent were administrative errors while only 32 percent were substantive errors. Real estate practice, in contrast, involved only 15 percent administrative errors, but 57 percent substantive errors. In family practice, 27 percent of all errors were related to client relations. None of these results seem out of the ordinary. An analysis of the corporate and business practice, however, reveals that here 50 percent of the claims made are premised on substantive errors. "Intentional wrongs" showed up most often in claims related to criminal defense practice. If a similar study were to be conducted today, I believe the results would be similar.

Now let's examine the size of the law firm and its relationship to the claims submitted. It is interesting that the *Profile* concludes that 78.5 percent of all claims reported are from firms of five or fewer attorneys. In fact, 34.9 percent of all the claims are linked to sole practitioners, while only 2.2 percent of the reported claims were under policies covering thirty or more lawyers. It should be noted that the study points out that "Two major insurers of large law firms have not reported data to the ABA [American Bar Association]." The *Profile* says that most of these losses probably fall within the self-insurance or deductible limits of the larger firms. My experience has been that these large firms cover a substantial part of their losses or maintain comparatively high deductibles. As a consequence, it is impossible to collect statistics for analysis from these firms without visiting each one.

The *Profile,* citing the Curran Report, (see p. 5) concluded that sole practitioners represented 48.6 percent of all practicing lawyers were responsible for 34.9 percent of all claims. Firms of two to five lawyers represented 22.4 percent of all practitioners and accounted for 43.6 percent of all claims. Firms of six or more, while representing 28.9 percent of all practitioners accounted for 21.5 percent of all claims. (See *Profile,* pp. 20 et seq.). A further analysis of the alleged group error by law firm size is interesting for any analysis of legal malpractice.

Administrative errors accounted for 25.8 percent of all claims; and these types of errors represented 27 percent of all sole practitioner claims, 26.1 percent of all claims against firms of two to five people, and 24.6 percent of all claims for firms of six to thirty. In firms with more than thirty members, only 13.3 percent of the claims were based on administrative errors. Substantive errors, which represent 43.7 percent of all claims, were consistent throughout all categories. Client-related errors were also consistent in that they represented 16.3 percent of all claims, except for firms with more than thirty members. In that firm size category, there was only a 14.8 percent rate of client related errors. Intentional wrongs, which made up 11.6 percent of all claims, were generally consistent except in firms of thirty or more members. In this category, intentional wrongs made up 23.3 percent (23.3%) of all claims. The *Profile* concludes that the administrative errors decrease with firm size and intentional wrongs increase with firm size. (See *Profile*, p. 22.)

In analyzing the relationship between error, the area of law, and firm size, it is interesting that the *Profile* indicates that, for real estate, large firms showed the lowest probability of administrative error. An interesting result is that the medium-large law firm (six to thirty) had the highest probability of intentional error, and the lowest probability of substantive error. The correlation between the size of a firm and the nature and incidence of claims should be further investigated to determine the cause of this result.

When one analyzes the relationship between the two factors — years admitted to the Bar and percent of claims, the results appear predictable. The Curran Report seems especially exact in its analysis of the lawyer population. Of all claims reported, only 4 percent arose from lawyers with fewer than three years of experience. In contrast, lawyers with over ten years of experience accounted for about 66 percent of the claims. Lawyers who had practiced between four and ten years accounted for the remaining 30 percent of claims. In analyzing the years admitted versus errors, the *Profile* concludes that "No relational trend is apparent between percentage of alleged error and percentage of experienced lawyers for any of the error groups." (See *Profile*, p. 34.)

While the attorney admitted to the Bar less than four years earlier has the highest probability of administrative error, he or she is less likely to provoke a client-related error. The personal injury lawyers have the highest probability of making errors in substantive or client-related matters. The *Profile* also comments on the fact that in collections and bankruptcy, the experienced lawyers have the highest probability of error, while the middle group has the lowest. In corporate and business organizations "the inexperienced lawyers had the lowest probability of error in the substantive law, but the highest probability in the administrative and client related areas." In family law, administrative errors increase with years of experience. The inexperienced lawyers, by contrast, have the highest probability of substantive error, but the lowest probability in client related and intentional wrongs. The study also concludes that for criminal lawyers, years admitted does not seem to have an effect on errors other than client related ones, where the inexperienced lawyers have the highest probability and the experienced lawyers have the lowest probability of error. Errors in estate practice demonstrate that younger lawyers have a higher probability of administrative error and a lower probability of client-related errors, but for substantive and intentional wrongs, the years since admission did not affect the frequency of errors.

Another area in the *Profile* report involved the Data Center's compilation of information about clients versus non-clients who were claimants in legal malpractice actions. Clients — including those receiving free legal service, members of prepaid legal plans, and others — made up 87 percent of all claims. The study concludes, "For the client related group the percent of errors decreases with increasing non-client activity, an expected result since thereby client activity is reduced." (See *Profile,* p. 48.) Claims of intentional wrongs increase with non-client activity. The study concluded, however, that non-client claims were dramatically higher for intentional wrongs. "This is an expected result since lawyers are generally not liable to non-clients for negligence." (See *Profile,* p. 48.) Experience suggests that the frequency of claims brought by non-clients should have increased dramatically since the study was completed. With greater non-client awareness of legal malpractice, the study's conclusions in this area may now be challenged, particularly when one examines the case law throughout the United States.

Another area that has shown a dramatic increase in claims since the conclusion of the study is fee disputes. Of the initial claims studied, 6.8 percent arose after an attempt to collect a fee. Family law accounted for 19.3 percent of the total; corporate and business, 8.8 percent; criminal, 7.6 percent; collection and bankruptcy, 7.5 percent. I suspect that, today, the percentage of claims in which a counterclaim was filed in response to a lawyer's effort to collect a fee is substantially higher.

Finally, the study analyzes closed claims. It concludes that in 67 percent of the cases, no payment was made to the plaintiff, 49.8 percent of the claims were abandoned, and 17 percent were dismissed. Settlement payments were made in 32 percent of the cases and 38 percent of these payments (12 percent of all closed claims) followed initiation of a suit. There is no question that today plaintiffs win more often than they appear to from the claims analyzed. This conclusion is further supported by a report that the incidence of legal malpractice claims increased 300 percent from 1980 to 1985. The percentage of claims closed without payment decreased from 75 percent in 1980 to 60 percent in 1985. (See Remarks of Robert T. Reid, "Professional Liability Insurance Market: The Company's View," DRI Defense Practice Seminar, *Professional Liability 1986:*

Legal Development and Trends, Insuring the Professional and the Economics of Litigation, September 18-19, 1986, Denver, CO., p. J-4). My experience has been that the entire legal malpractice environment has changed. Now it not only favors the plaintiff in a technical, legal sense, but in a pragmatic sense as well.

The study also reveals that in 1 percent of total claims resulting in judgment for the plaintiff, payment was made. Also it appears as though 19 percent of the fee collection claims resulted in payment. The *Profile* attributes this difference to the fact that one-third of fee collection claims are ultimately dismissed.

Another part of the *Profile* analyzed the cost of closing a claim. While the dollar figures are outdated, some trends may still be valid. For example, the percentage of closed claims over one hundred thousand dollars was only 1 percent. Whereas 66 percent of all closed claims represented from zero to one-thousand-dollar payments, 85 percent of all claims are five thousand dollars. What still may be true today is that 20 percent of all administrative errors resulted in losses of over ten thousand dollars, while only 4 percent of all other claims resulted in losses of more than ten thousand dollars.

EXAMPLES OF LEGAL MALPRACTICE
SOCK AROUND THE CLOCK: BILLING ABUSES

THERE IS one universal opinion about how lawyers bill their clients: LAWYERS CHARGE TOO MUCH! Regardless of whether you are part of an upper, middle, or lower income family, you probably agree that lawyers overcharge. Related to this perception of overcharging is the issue of access to the judicial system. That's the real issue that demands exploration. The poor may have some access through the use of public defenders, the Legal Aid Society, or similar programs. Even with the help of these programs, however, the poor don't always have access to the court system, particularly in view of the recent cutbacks of these programs. Middle income clients rarely have access to the judicial system. They suffer the most from overcharging, because a lawyer can affect their finances for the rest of their lives. The rich, while they have access to the courts, are also overcharged for their lawyers' services. Lawyers look to some wealthy clients as "annuities" for the senior partners.

Today, lawyers probably make more money than they ever have. Like other professionals, lawyers charge astronomical rates to maintain not only their own lifestyles, but also to meet the increasing expenses involved in maintaining a law office.

Let's look at the finances facing an attorney who works a forty-hour week, only takes a two-week vacation, and is in the office every business day, without taking off any other time for vacations, holidays, religious leave, illness. If we assume the attorney works fifty weeks at forty hours per week, we know the attorney works a maximum of two thousand hours. These are all the hours an attorney can possibly bill for. Some large firms, however, require associates to bill to twenty-five hundred hours per year. This requirement is a large part of the problem that can be called attorney misconduct in billing procedures. In any event, the attorney has a limited number of hours he or she can bill for. We all know that not every single moment of the attorney's time is billable. There are occasions when the attorney socializes, has lunch, or engages in other activities that do not result in actual billable time. There is great pressure on today's attorney to, nevertheless, bill for this time, owing to a combination of law office expenses and greed. In other words, the attorney bills the client dishonestly for hours never worked.

The real problem that this billing misconduct creates is that the average middle income citizen can no longer afford access to the court system. By closely examining law office expenses, it's easy to see why most Americans cannot afford to use a lawyer's services and, in turn, cannot find their way into court. Something must be done about this American tragedy.

These billing abuses are not the only abuses rampant within the system. For example, while retainer agreements should be part of every lawyer-client relationship, often they are not. Retainer agreements are contracts between lawyers and clients that state the fees and clarify other aspects of the lawyer-client relationship. If a retainer agreement is not signed, an attorney may take advantage of a client, especially in terms of fees and billings. For example, an attorney who needs an immediate financial fix might excessively charge a client with "deep pockets." Furthermore, if an associate attorney in a large law firm needs to beef up his billing to meet the "quotas," a prime target is always the client who has sufficient means to support prolonged litigation. The message to the young associate is "bill the file" or "charge the client." By establishing the fees and billing procedure before litigation, a retainer agreement discourages this kind of legal misconduct.

Let's take as an example a case I am presently involved with. This was a divorce case which came to my attention because it involved a legal malpractice lawsuit. A man of substantial means went to his lawyer, who was recognized as one of the leading matrimonial lawyers in the State of New Jersey. The client thought he was retaining the services of an expert in divorce. The wife and the husband were about to settle the case for an agreed-upon amount, in exchange for the wife's share of the couple's property. According to my client, his attorney discouraged him from negotiating with the wife and insisted the matter be tried before a judge in order to save the husband a "considerable sum of money." Two years later the case was settled with the husband paying the wife a sum which was equal to the previously discussed settlement amount and, in addition, several hundred thousand dollars representing legal costs and expenses for both the husband as well as the wife. In other words, the husband ended up paying not only what the wife had originally asked for but, in addition, he paid for two years of unnecessary legal fees and expenses.

Another example of a legal fee abuse involves a client who retained an attorney to handle a dispute between a landlord and his tenant. The tenant had a right to purchase the house and a small business on the property. When the client, who was the tenant, signed an agreement with the attorney, the client was unaware that he was assigning his rights to that property to his own attorney. When the attorney wanted to get paid, he went to court and got a judge to sign an order transferring the property from the client to the lawyer. The attorney turned the property over to his partner's wife, who was a realtor. She sold it to an acquaintance of theirs. This was all done within one day. Then, under the attorney's direction, the sheriff forced the client out of his own home. This story was told to me by my own client. In other words, the client's own attorney ordered the sheriff to evict the client from the client's own home. The attorney general's office telephoned me and asked me to consider suing the lawyer for legal malpractice.

The horror stories go on and on of lawyers who abuse their clients by fee gouging. Regrettably, the people least able to afford attorney fees are those hardest pressed to pay them. If they cannot afford to pay the fees, they are denied access to the courts. The rich often find that they are paying for the education of a herd of associates who work on each and every file. What does this mean? Attorneys hire new lawyers as associates. These associates, who work for a smaller salary, are required to bill substantially. They are, in fact, learning the practice of law at the expense of the clients. This intolerable situation must be changed. Clients must know up front how much they are going to pay for legal services, and under what circumstances they are going to pay for those services. Clients should not pay to educate an attorney's associates. Clients should also be aware that "conferences" among attorneys contribute to these questionable billing practices. Some attorneys will meet associate lawyers for lunch and charge the client for conferring on the client's file. It seems that there is an endless number of abusive billing practices.

Attorneys' abusive billing practices could be detailed chapter by chapter. Instead I'd like to mention one last example involving an attorney who took on a matter that was eventually dismissed due to the attorney's negligence. The attorney was to file an answer to "interrogatories" (written questions which one party sends to the other party to be answered, in writing, by the recipient), but failed to do so. When the attorney made an application to the court to restore the matter or, in essence, to say he was sorry for his error, he billed the client for this service. In reality, the attorney was actually double-billing the client. This practice not only cheats the client, it also makes the client financially responsible for the attorney's misconduct. Not only will the client's case be prejudiced, but the client also has to pay for being prejudiced! Another variation on this theme involves an attorney who has a case dismissed for negligent delay in handling a case. The attorney makes an appeal to the appellate court. Then the attorney charges the client for handling the appeal, which was necessary only because of the attorney's negligent delay.

Another problem that should be addressed when discussing billing procedures is that lawyers are notorious for abusing the legal system. More often than not, clients are the victims of attorneys' inability to sit down and resolve matters. Often, in fact, attorneys create problems for their clients rather than solutions. Lawyers are, for the most part, problem creators and not problem solvers. Often, attorneys will take advantage of a wealthy client and will go to court and fight over each and every issue, no matter how trivial. Most of the time it is a question of lawyers' egos being boosted at the clients' expense. Lawyers will fight with one another, fail to communicate with each other, and refuse to accept reasonable prospects of third-party mediation or alternative dispute resolution solely because this would lessen the likelihood of the attorneys getting paid enormous sums for legal services. If the case settles, the lawyer must stop billing. Lawyers charge for every aspect of services rendered. For example, if an attorney has to make an appearance in court, and there are ten other cases in which that attorney or his law firm is making an appearance, in the same court, the client undoubtedly will pay for each and every hour of court time, instead of a fair proportion or pro rata share of the attorney's time involvement. If the attorney needs to clarify an issue, the attorney will not hesitate to personally perform a service, like a trip to the courthouse, even though that service could be done by someone else at less expense to the client. Instead of sending an associate or paralegal, whose time is less expensive, the attorney often takes the simple tasks upon him or herself, and charges the client for the time spent.

All of these abuses add up to a legal system that is out of control from a financial standpoint. In essence, the lawyers are pricing themselves out of business. In certain cases, the license to practice law is a license to steal.

WHEN YOUR HOME CAN BE YOUR DUNGEON: REAL ESTATE TRANSACTIONS

TRADITIONALLY, PART of the American dream has been to own your own home. When an attorney is called in to handle the transaction, that American dream can turn into a nightmare. In most states, lawyers are involved on behalf of the buyers and sellers of residential property; on behalf of the lending institutions; and possibly on behalf of the title company. One would think that with all the lawyers involved in this type of transaction that it would go smoothly. Nothing could be further from the truth.

In 1986, the American Bar Association Committee on Professional Responsibility reported that almost one-fourth of all reported claims against lawyers involved real estate transactions. (See *Profile,* p. 8.) Therefore, if you are a victim of legal malpractice, there is a one-in-four chance that it will involve the purchase or sale of real estate. Typically, a buyer of real estate hires a lawyer to draft or review the contract, to purchase property, to advise and inform the client as to problems, and, close the title to that property. Unfortunately, many times the attorney will close the real estate transaction without discovering that there are liens against the property. That is, the attorney doesn't find out about the interests of other persons in the property before closing of title. If the attorney doesn't discover these liens against the property, the buyer then purchases the property subject to those liens. In some cases that means that the buyer does not own the property after he or she has paid for it! Rather, the person with the lien has an interest or right in the property that may come before the interests of the buyer. For example, consider a person who has prior rights to a right of way across the property. Many times a utility company may have the right to go into the property and place utility lines. If the attorney doesn't point out that lien, the buyer may later discover trucks in front of the house, digging utility lines across the property. Or, even worse, there may be a prior owner of a recorded interest in the land who shows up at the property unannounced. Or perhaps some other party had a prior deed to the land

and that party never signed off before the new buyers purchased the house. That would mean someone else had a greater interest than the buyers of the property. Finally, you might purchase a house and find someone else living there with you as a partner if your attorney fails to properly read and interpret the documents before you buy the house.

Another example of legal malpractice involving the purchase of real estate is illustrated in a case I was involved in. The clients were buying a two-family house. They checked with the township and determined it was in an area zoned for two-family residences. The buyers then got a mortgage, knowing that they were going to rent part of the house (the other residence) to pay off the mortgage. They knew that they would take in just enough rent to pay the mortgage. After a while, one of the township officials visited them. Evidently, two-family houses were not permitted in that zone, only one-family houses. The official then ordered the parties to evict the tenant on the basis that renting part of the house was an unlawful use of the premises. Of course, if the tenant were evicted, the owner would, perhaps, no longer be able to pay the mortgage. This could mean that the house would be placed in jeopardy of foreclosure. The lesson to be learned from this example is that the buyer of a house must understand that there must be a complete investigation into all possible problems before the closing of title.

One last example involves outright wrongdoing by the attorney. Let's say that you are purchasing a new house, and give your lawyer money to pay off the mortgage and note on the house you're selling. You present the attorney with a check for $100,000 to pay off the mortgage and note, so the old house can be sold free and clear. If that attorney absconds, or is negligent and does not pay off the existing mortgage and note, a lien remains on the house. The new buyers would then be responsible for paying off that lien; in other words, even though the buyers had paid the full purchase price they would still be required to pay off the existing lien if they wanted clear title. Another variation on this theme involves an attorney who, by error, does not learn that there is an existing mortgage on a house before he allows the buyers to buy it. If the buyers purchase the house and are unaware that the seller has an existing mortgage on it, the buyers could be liable for that mortgage. While the buyers might be able to sue a seller, in many instances the seller has left for parts unknown. Of course, a buyer's purchasing title insurance can remove much of the uncertainty of hidden mortgages and liens; unfortunately, this insurance will not protect against the unscrupulous real estate attorney.

CONFLICTS OF INTEREST

CONFLICTS OF interest are common in real estate transactions. House buyers often rely on the broker or real estate agent to recommend an attorney to handle the transaction. When this occurs there is automatically a conflict of interest, at least in appearance, if not in reality. Theoretically, the lawyer should vigorously negotiate on behalf of the client. In many real estate transactions, however, the lawyer is more concerned with pleasing the real estate agent or broker, to get more referrals. As a consequence, the client may not get uncompromised legal advice. Rather, the attorney may be attempting to satisfy the broker. I have witnessed a substantial number of cases in which the attorney compromised the client's interests in order to satisfy the real estate broker or agent.

Another kind of conflict of interest involves an attorney who represents both sides of a transaction. As incredible as this may sound, in many real estate transactions the same attorney represents both buyer and seller. To avoid ethical problems, the attorney has both the buyer and seller sign a letter authorizing the lawyer to act for both sides. Even with such a letter, however, this practice seems to encourage negligence. At no time should an attorney act on behalf of both buyer and seller. There should always be an independent attorney for each side, even if it's only to review documents to insure that they are fair. The purchase of a house is usually one of the most important and certainly one of the most expensive investments that any of us will make during our lifetimes. We want to be certain that legal negligence doesn't turn this pursuit of the American dream into a nightmare.

ADDING INSULT TO INJURY: PERSONAL INJURY CASES

THE MOST common example of legal malpractice in handling personal injury cases involves an attorney's ignorance of or inability to abide by time limits that apply to the case. What do I mean by this? The most obvious example is an attorney who has a certain amount of time to file a lawsuit on behalf of a victim of, for example, a car accident. This time period is commonly referred to as "the statute of limitations." If the attorney fails to start a lawsuit within the statute of limitations, the client will be forever prevented from bringing suit. In most of these situations, attorneys simply defraud the client by not telling the client the truth: the attorney failed to file a lawsuit within the time allowed. A conspiracy of silence is obvious in this area of the practice of law. In many instances, the attorneys will conceal and deny the fact that they have failed to file the lawsuit within the time period.

Another example of malpractice involving time limitations occurs when an attorney fails to perform discovery, which means interrogatories or depositions according to a schedule imposed by the court or the rules of the court. The attorney's failure to answer interrogatories or to produce a client for deposition, or failure to timely file claims against governmental institutions or entities, for example, may cause the client to be barred from reopening the case after it is dismissed. If an attorney representing a defendant fails to abide by these discovery rules, the answer to the plaintiff's complaint will be stricken. Other cases may involve accident reconstruction experts or experts in financial, medical, or legal malpractice. There may be time limitations for providing reports from these experts. The frequency with which lawyers conceal such time-related errors creates a crisis. Lawyers lie to their clients. They rarely admit their errors.

Another prominent area of attorney errors or omissions in connection with personal injury cases involves inadequate representation, and representation without informed participation by the client. These two situations go hand in hand. The attorney handling a particular personal injury case is often not familiar with personal injury practice. As a consequence, the attorney may settle a case either without the client's consent, or without the client being fully informed of the potential for recovery. Time after time I have heard from victims of legal malpractice involved in personal injury cases in which the attorney settles the case without the client's involvement or consent. After the fact, the attorney then turns to the client and says that the claim has been settled. The lawyer treats the case as though the case belongs to him or her and not to the client. The client must always remember that an attorney will have many other cases to handle after this particular case is over. In contrast, however, this may be the only chance the client has for recovery. For that reason, the client must be fully aware of and protective of his or her own case and must alert the attorney to the importance of keeping the client informed at every stage of the proceedings.

TILL DOLLARS DO YOU PART:
DIVORCE MATTERS

A CLIENT is especially vulnerable to being a victim of legal malpractice during a divorce proceeding. For many reasons, the client tends to rely almost exclusively on the attorney's advice. Unfortunately, I see more complaints made against divorce lawyers than any other type of lawyer. This is because, soon after the divorce, when emotions have calmed, the clients re-evaluate their positions and reality sets in. And it is at this point that the client usually begins to complain about the attorney's conduct, the settlement, or the result of the divorce. In one case an attorney failed to make adequate discovery of the husband's assets. Later, after the husband died, the wife learned of a very large estate he had left to his new family. She then wanted to sue her former lawyer for negligence in handling her divorce.

In addition, in divorce proceedings, lawyers tend to overcharge. In these cases attorneys often engage in malicious and senseless litigation, mere one-upmanship, all at the client's expense. Clients are charged for divorce litigation. Right from the beginning of the case, the client should determine what the realistic prospects of recovery are, and then evaluate the case from a strictly economic standpoint. Customarily, the only parties that benefit from contested litigation are the lawyers. In divorce proceedings, I recommend that clients monitor the attorneys' conduct even more than usual. All too often I hear complaints that the other party hid income during the course of the divorce. In the past, the majority of these complaints have come from women. Today more men, however, have begun to complain. I always advise clients, whether they are male or female, to monitor their attorney to ensure that all important witnesses are called to trial. In particular, focus on those witnesses who would know about the spouse's income and expenses. That is to say, where and how the spouse spends money for necessities and luxuries should be known; otherwise, the client does not have all the information available to make a proper judgment. Until that information is collected, no client is in a position to properly evaluate his or her case and make an informed judgment whether to settle or to try the case.

TO CATCH A THIEF: CRIMINAL CASES

THE ATTORNEY defending criminal cases is the one least likely to face a legal malpractice claim for negligence in handling the matter. This is probably not because these attorney commit less malpractice than other attorneys, but rather because the client, a criminal, will probably receive the least sympathy from a jury when complaining of legal malpractice. I have often been asked to sue lawyers who have pressured their clients into pleading guilty when the clients are not guilty to begin with. I have heard of cases where attorneys have failed to file motions to suppress evidence in criminal proceedings. While the criminals in these cases may not have been sympathetic figures, the criminal, nevertheless, is entitled to the same quality of representation as any other person. It doesn't matter whether or not the individual uses a public defender, private counsel, or someone assigned by the court. Customarily, in cases where states require *pro bono* work, that is, where the attorney is obligated to do some work on behalf of the poor or indigent, at reduced or no fees, the attorney is more likely to commit legal malpractice. In many cases, the *pro bono* attorney is inept in handling the kinds of cases assigned because the attorney has no particular experience in the particular legal field. These situations generate the overwhelming majority of legal malpractice cases in the criminal defense area. Incredibly, these victims of legal malpractice are, however, the least likely to retain an attorney to bring a legal malpractice case.

The criminal is far more vulnerable to the legal system because of the trauma of being accused or, even worse, being found guilty of a crime. Serving time in jail is one of the most stressful human experiences. As a result of this stress, the individual charged with a crime may be misled by the attorney handling the defense. Many times the criminal defense attorney is not well seasoned, and struggles with the procedural requirements as well as with the factual complexities of the case. In many instances the defendant relies on the advice of the attorney in entering a plea of guilty to a lesser crime. The client is then shocked by the resulting jail sentence. In fact, in may cases, bail is revoked and the defendant is led off to jail on the spot! In one case, the defendant paid the attorney $100,000 just to plea guilty to a crime he did not commit. The defendant had no idea he was going to go to prison and, when he was carted off to jail, his application for a stay of sentence was denied. As a result, before appeals could be heard, the defendant had already spent a substantial amount of time in jail.

When referring to the phrase "to catch a thief," in many cases we're never really quite sure whether it's the attorney or the criminal defendant who is the thief. The criminal defendant needs to know what the attorney's services include, and the defendant must be informed of the charges for fees and expenses that will be made for those services. The criminal defendant should also be aware of what motions may be filed and discovery obtained in the defense of the case. All this information should be provided to the defendant but it rarely is. Copies of all discovery, including grand jury minutes, expert testimony, recreation of crimes, and a list of witnesses should be provided. In almost every one of these cases, an investigator should be hired or assigned, but usually is not. Lists of witnesses should be prepared and the witnesses interviewed by both sides, but this also is frequently left undone. All these factors determine whether or not the attorney has competently handled the criminal case. Most courts will not reverse a conviction solely on the basis of an attorney's conduct unless it can be shown that the attorney's misconduct was a material factor in bringing about the defendant's conviction. As a consequence, those charged with crimes sometimes do not get the full benefit of our system of justice.

GIVING YOU THE BUSINESS: BUSINESS MATTERS & COMMERCIAL TRANSACTIONS

STATISTICS SHOW us that many businesses fail. From what I've seen, many businesses fail because of the inadequacy of the attorney representing the individual business owner. I have seen attorneys literally ruin businesses by not being well versed in a particular area. For example, consider an attorney who is not familiar with environmental regulations. He closes a deal for the sale of a business; his client is the purchaser. The client later discovers there are hazardous wastes on the property. I am involved in a case like this right now and, as incredible as it may sound, if there are hazardous wastes on the property, it could cost more than one million dollars to clean up the site. This is obviously a disaster to a small businessperson.

There are other instances in which the business seller is represented by an attorney. The buyer wants to purchase the business with no collateral. I've seen numerous cases where the seller's attorney either does not require collateral or provide the seller with a security interest in the business. In other words, there is no lien on equipment or personal property. If the buyer defaults and simply does not pay the seller, the seller is at the mercy of the court system and must file a law suit on the promissory note. Without the security of liens and mortgages, the seller is left without any remedy other than spending years in court trying to get paid or get back the business. I have also been involved in consultation in which the seller's attorney in a business sale transaction failed to file the security lien in time. If the security lien is not filed in time, it may not be valid. As a result of not having a valid security interest, if the buyer defaults, the seller is again without an adequate remedy other than a lawsuit on the promissory note.

In many instances, the attorney handling a business transaction is basically unfamiliar with the terms of the sale. Because of the complexity in this area of the law, particularly when it involves stock transactions, partnership arrangements, or closely held corporations, the client ultimately becomes the victim of legal malpractice because the attorney simply does not know all of the consequences of the transaction. The lawyer may not be familiar with tax considerations in the sale or purchase of a business. Although this may appear to be a minor consideration, it ultimately could have ruinous effects. I have been involved in transactions where the attorneys did not consider prior tax liens on the business, or didn't perform searches to adequately discover what the tax liens might be. As a consequence of this type of error, the buyer may then end up buying a business burdened by tax liens far exceeding the value of the business. As a result, when money later comes into the business, the Internal Revenue Service or the state tax people will be at the door, ready to be the first to collect. Deprived of income, the business will probably fail. Later, when the attorney is questioned about his negligence in mishandling the transaction, most likely the lawyer will be hard pressed to explain why the tax situation was not considered and dealt with.

A PENNY SAVED, A DOLLAR LOST: THE LAWYER AS AN INVESTMENT ADVISOR

ONE ASPECT of legal practice that never ceases to amaze me is the frequency with which people entrust lawyers with substantial sums of money as financial advisors. Individuals who have worked all their lives to save money often place sizeable sums of money in their attorneys' hands. The attorneys have the absolute authority to invest the money as they see fit. Nowhere is it written that a lawyer is qualified as an investment advisor. Nowhere does it say that a lawyer should have the authority to provide a client with investment recommendations. Yet because they are in a position of trust, some lawyers find themselves immersed in the lucrative business of investment counselor. Often, lawyers abuse this privilege of handling clients' money by having one hand in the till. What I mean by this is that many attorneys take illegal kickbacks and referral fees from investment and financial planners. This means that if you entrust a lawyer with an investment, the money may end up in the wrong hands. For their recommendations, the lawyers may receive kickbacks; for their trust, the clients risk losing their investments. Usually, this type of transaction involves Security and Exchange violations. Even worse (from the client's point of view), the attorney may reap additional benefits. Often, lawyers are rewarded for their recommendations by the investment and financial planners, referring other clients to these lawyers.

In all too many cases, I've seen attorneys not only mismanage funds, but also steal funds from clients. The client relies on the attorney to provide sound investment advice, but the lawyer abuses that trust by mismanaging or pilfering the funds. Often the attorney actually has a personal interest in the transaction. Frequently the attorney acts as a director or officer of a corporate investment group, and encourages investors or clients to invest with the attorney to ensure the financial success of the investment group. By not disclosing his own interest in the transaction, the attorney engages in a conflict of interest. In many instances, especially in real estate, the attorney is entitled to referral fees for his recommendation, but rarely discloses this fact to the client. In other instances, the attorney may very well have an interest in a real estate transaction, and may encourage the client to invest in that real estate, but fails to disclose to the client that he is actually a partner in the transaction or will benefit directly from the client's investment. Too often an attorney takes a client's money without the client's knowledge or consent and invests it for the attorney's own use. When the lawyer does this, there is a clear conflict of interest. More often than not, the attorney mismanages the money and ends up losing all or at least a good part of it. This conduct is obviously detrimental to the client. One very real concern for the victim of this type of legal malpractice is that the lawyer may not be covered by legal malpractice insurance to pay for such an infraction. If the investment scheme was fraudulent, or if the misconduct involved an area of the law that was specifically excluded by the legal malpractice insurance policy, there may not be any insurance coverage for the attorney and therefore no money for the victim. The lawyer often lacks sufficient personal funds to compensate the victim for the losses. The victim may have to look to a state Bar program if one is available, for compensation.

I always recommend that clients secure the advice of independent investment counselors, experts, or an independent legal opinion before investing with a lawyer.

AFTER YOU'VE GONE, THE LAWYER LIVES ON: HANDLING WILLS & ESTATE PLANNING

THE LAWYER who draws a will on behalf of a client and designates him or herself as a trustee, executor, or beneficiary, undoubtedly faces a conflict of interest in the preparation of the will itself. I have always advised lawyers that, if they are going to be the principal party in a will or a named party in the will transaction, the lawyer should send the client for advice to an independent attorney. Unfortunately, most attorneys exert undue influence on the party for whom they are drafting the will. The attorney is guilty of legal malpractice with a conflict of interest when the lawyer seeks to influence the party from whom he or she is drawing the will into naming the lawyer as a beneficiary of the estate. For example, imagine a will of a person with a sizeable estate. Once the attorney has positioned him or herself as a trustee of the estate, the attorney is then entitled to substantial commissions because of his or her work as a trustee. In many cases, I've seen the attorney designate him or herself as beneficiary of a will. Clearly, in that instance, the attorney is benefiting monetarily from the drafting of that document. In those situations, I always recommend independent legal advice to the client to ensure impartiality of adivce on the part of the lawyer drafting the document.

Also take the example of the attorney who represents one of the potential beneficiaries of the will. In many cases, the attorney draws the will and ensures that that one beneficiary receives a disproportionate amount of rights from the will. If the attorney clearly favors one of the beneficiaries (probably someone he or she represented in the past), there will automatically be a conflict of interest and unfair influence in connection with the drafting of the document. It is these errors of judgment and self-serving advice that attorneys make on a regular basis which give rise to claims of malpractice.

Even more basic is the fact that an attorney may not know all the rules governing the execution of a will. The attorney, moreover, might not be aware of all of the tax considerations involved in drafting such an instrument. These factors could have a dramatic effect upon how the property is ultimately distributed after death. For example, let's say you wanted to exclude certain members of your immediate family from receiving anything under your will. If the attorney does not specifically address the exclusion of a particular individual from the will in that instrument, this person may come forward to argue that there was an error made in the drafting of the document. If the lawyer simply stated this individual was specifically excluded from receiving anything from the will, the estate could be spared the spending of many dollars in senseless lawyers' fees for litigation after the death of the testator or testatrix.

Another consideration in the area of wills and estates is that no one wants to share an estate with the taxing authority. If taxes may legitimately be avoided, there should be adequate advice governing how the will should be drawn to do so. Without that advice, the document will be subject to additional penalties and taxes that otherwise could be saved by rendering proper advice. There are not many general practitioners who are experts in the tax law.

Therefore, if taxes are an important consideration, one may need an expert in tax law to draft the will in order to maximize the estate and income tax benefits. This can save valuable tax dollars when the estate is distributed. Generally keep in mind the rule: "let your will be without controversy lest your attorney be your heir." ≡

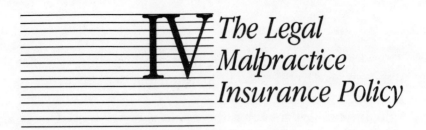

IV The Legal Malpractice Insurance Policy

THE OCCURRENCE VS. THE CLAIMS MADE POLICY: THE DIFFERENCE IN INSURANCE

ONE THRESHOLD question in the evaluation of legal malpractice is whether or not there is legal malpractice insurance for the loss. In order to determine whether or not there is insurance coverage, it is first necessary to analyze the legal malpractice insurance policy. The form that is now universally accepted as the basic policy in lawyers' professional liability insurance is known as the "claims made policy." The claims made policy differs from the traditional lawyers' professional liability insurance form which is commonly referred to as the "occurrence insurance policy." We are all accustomed to dealing with the traditional policy which provides for insurance coverage for the "occurrences" which take place during the policy year. Conversely, while there are a number of variations to the claims made policy, its principle feature is that it provides insurance coverage for claims that are made against the insured attorney and reported to the insurance company during the policy year in which the insurance coverage was secured. It is important to remember that there are wide variations in both types of insurance policies. Not surprisingly, there are a number of significant legal issues attached to each form which impact on claims being submitted for legal malpractice. In order to understand the following analysis of the claims made policy, it is

50

important to look to the development of the claims made policy form in the history of legal malpractice insurance.

The development of the claims made insurance policy occurred primarily as a result of the unpredictability of underwriting losses in connection with lawyers' malpractice insurance. Actually the development of the claims made policy paralleled the development of all professional liability lines. The claims made policy allows for predictability of losses whereas its predecessor policy, namely, the occurrence policy, prevented the insurance industry from anticipating what its ultimate loss would be for writing lawyers' professional liability. As a consequence, the insurance industry devised the claims made policy form to forecast what the losses may be and thereby determine a rate structure which maintains profitability in lawyers' professional liability insurance.

Let's examine two basic examples as they apply to the occurrence versus claims made policy forms. As noted, the occurrence policy will generally provide insurance coverage for occurrences or accidents which take place within the year in which insurance coverage is purchased. For example, let's assume an attorney purchased professional liability insurance coverage from January 1, 1976 to December 31, 1976. During this calendar year, the attorney fails to file a claim within the applicable statute of limitations. While there are other considerations than the acts which led to the ultimate event or the failure on the part of the attorney to file the claim within the statute of limitations, the real error occurred in allowing the statute to expire during the 1976 calendar year. Under the traditional notions of an occurrence policy form, the attorney would indeed have insurance coverage for this act. It's important to note that there is insurance coverage for the act regardless of when the insured notified his insurance carrier of his act, error, or omission, subject to certain limitations. In this case the act or event was the failure to file the personal injury case on behalf of the client within the applicable statute of limitations. On preliminary examination, one might ask, Why would a system which insures an event or an occurrence during a policy year provide unpredictable losses for the insurance industry? The answer is the basic premise of the occurrence form. While the insured's error may have occurred during the term of the policy, the insurance carrier may not know about the loss until a substantial amount of time has elapsed. In other words, the insurance carrier may not be informed of the loss until many years later. This is what is commonly referred to as "tail" coverage. The insured attorney is obligated to report the loss as soon as practicable. In most jurisdictions, however, the insurance carrier is obligated to pay the loss regardless of when the insured provides notice to the insurance carrier, unless the insurance carrier is able to show appreciable prejudice in the insured's late reporting. In many cases in lawyers' professional liability, the insured attorney may not even learn about the loss until a substantial amount of time has passed after the event. Let's assume for a moment that the attorney insured under a lawyer's professional liability insurance policy, claims that he or she simply misfiled the client's case into a closed claim file. That client may not have contacted the attorney until several years after the statute of limitations expired to determine the status of the claim. Therefore, the attorney may not report the claim until a substantial amount of time has lapsed, long after the expiration of the policy. It follows that, when the insurance industry sets the rates for any year, it actually does not know the essential statistics for the setting of a rate that is fair, equitable, and profitable.

It is stressed that this is a system that was devised in theory. As we will learn from later chapters, the reality of the development of the claims made policy is far different than its theoretical development.

With the development of the claims made policy came

variations to the pure claims made policy form. It is interesting that the claims made form has frequently been referred to as the "discovery" policy. While the claims made policy in its pure form was in fact a discovery policy, insurance carriers have implemented various forms of the claims made policy in an effort to restrict the coverage that may be available under its pure form. As a consequence of this effort, the validity of the claims made policy has been challenged in almost every jurisdiction. What we now find is a universal acceptance of the pure claims made policy. In its pure form it is been held not to be void against public policy or unconscionable, provided, however, that the claims made policy meets the reasonable expectations of an insured under a given lawyer's professional liability policy.

Let's survey the claims made policy in its various forms in an effort to analyze the status of the law today governing lawyers' professional liability policies. The most comprehensive survey of the law governing lawyers' professional liability claims made policy may be found in two companion cases that were decided by the New Jersey Supreme Court in 1985. The decisions are entitled *Zuckerman v. National Union Fire Insurance Company* 100 N.J. 304 (1985) and its companion case of *Sparks v. St. Paul Insurance Company,* 100 N.J. 324 (1985). An analysis of both of these cases provides a national perspective on the enforceability of claims made policies and its various forms. Preliminary to the discussion of both cases, I will illustrate the hybrid form claims made policy as it relates to these issues.

As we have already noted, the claims made policy in its pure form requires that a claim be made against an insured attorney during the policy term and that the claim be reported by the insured attorney to the insurance carrier during that same policy term. We refer to this as "the pure claims made policy" inasmuch as the standard form language in the insuring agreement requires both the report to the company and the claim being first made against the insured during the policy term. One hybrid form of claims made policy requires that not only the claim be first made against the insured and reported to the insurance carrier during the policy term, but also requires that the wrongful act or event occur as well during the policy period. These forms of hybrid claims made policies have been consistently voided by the courts on various different grounds and theories. As you can see from this type of hybrid claims made policy, it combines what would appear an occurrence and a claims made policy form to restrict coverage. Let's take our simple example of an attorney who fails to file a claim within the applicable statute of limitations. Under the terms and conditions of the hybrid claims made policy, the wrongful acts — which include the failure of the attorney to file within the applicable statute of limitations — would have to occur within the same policy term that a claim is made against the lawyer, and the lawyer would have to report the claim to the insurance carrier within the same policy term. Let's take another example —the attorney who misfiles his client file and does not discover that he has failed to file the action within the statute of limitations until a considerable amount of time has passed. Under the terms and conditions of this hybrid policy, the attorney would have no insurance coverage. Therefore, the "discovery" hybrid claims made policy would provide no insurance when the attorney finally became aware of the loss. For a summary of the overview of this dilemma, one only has to look to the New Jersey Supreme Court in the *Sparks* decision where the Court states, "We assume that there are vast numbers of professionals covered by 'claims made' policies who are unaware of the basic distinction between their policies and the traditional 'occurrence' policy" (*Sparks, supra,* at pages 340-341). It is clearly recognized that this area of professional liability insurance is one which requires expertise by the insured in order to properly understand all the aspects of coverage.

In the *Zuckerman* case, Justice Stein, writing for a unanimous Supreme Court, surveyed the development of the law of both the occurrence and the claims made policies and determined that the claims made policy issued to Zuckerman by National Union Fire Insurance Company did not violate public policy and therefore was enforceable. The policy issued to Zuckerman provided the pure claims made policy in that National Union provided coverage for claims first made against the insured and reported to the company during the policy period. The facts of the underlying case were common, at least in my experience in lawyers' malpractice claims. Zuckerman was insured continuously by National Union Fire Insurance Company from January 15, 1974 through February 25, 1982. Each policy was written annually under a claims made policy form. It allowed for retroactive coverage or for coverage for acts, errors, or omissions that occurred prior to the effective date of the inception of coverage, provided the following: insured had no prior knowledge or reason to know of the claim prior to the inception of the policy, and it was first made against the insured and reported to the company during the policy period. In June 1982, after a default was entered against Zuckerman (by a former client and after he had made efforts to settle the claim directly with the former client), the default was set aside and the Court allowed the filing of a third-party complaint against the alleged negligent party in the underlying action. In December 1982, the claim was first reported to the carrier, National Union Fire Insurance Company. National Union disclaimed coverage on the basis that the first notice to the company was made ten months after the expiration of the last policy period. Zuckerman filed suit against National Union on the basis of a wrongful disclaimer. The trial court granted summary judgment on the basis that National Union was not able to show prejudice in Zuckerman's failure to report the claim within the policy term. The Appellate Division in a divided opinion reversed the trial court's granting a summary judgment. Justice Stein in writing for the majority of the New Jersey Supreme Court held that the claims made policy was indeed enforceable in its pure form.

However, Justice Stein, when writing for the unanimous New Jersey Supreme Court in the companion case of *Sparks v. St. Paul Insurance Company,* reached a different result based on a variation of the pure claims made policy. The lawyers' professional liability insurance that was at issue in *Sparks* involved a policy written by St. Paul Insurance for a lawyer by the name of Guarriello. The policy of insurance incepted in 1976 and was renewed until terminated in January 1980 for nonpayment of premium. The policy form was a claims made policy in that it provided for coverage for claims first made within the policy term, but did not provide retroactive coverage for acts, errors, or omissions which occurred prior to the effective date of the first policy. In other words, if a claim was first made against Guarriello arising out of an event, conduct, or an occurrence which happened prior to the first policy of insurance, there would be no coverage according to the terms and conditions of this policy. The policy also provided for extended reporting endorsement, which allows for an extension of the expiration of the policy date for the purposes of reporting claims. As a result of the negligence of Guarriello and his failure to answer a complaint filed by his former clients, a default judgment was entered against him. The policy was cancelled, according to St. Paul, on November 6, 1979, or as the Court held, January 21, 1980, but the Court pointed out that the effective date of cancellation was of no consequence. Counsel for the former clients placed St. Paul on notice of the claim between June and August 1980. St. Paul denied coverage by letter dated April 1981. Soon thereafter Mr. and Mrs. Sparks initiated a declaratory action seeking an adjudication that the policy issued to Guarriello should indeed pay the judgment which the clients in the underlying action had obtained against the attorney. Summary judgment was granted in favor of the clients and the Appellate Division affirmed, holding that the claims made policy was unenforceable as "violative of public policy." Justice Stein once again distinguished between the standard occurrence policy and the claims made policy and provided authority for each proposition. After reviewing the rationale of *Zuckerman,* the Court pointed out that in the *Sparks* case, the policy was not a pure claims made policy but a variation of the pure claims made policy that sought to restrict coverage. This evaluation indicates that the decision provides "neither the prospective coverage of a typical occurrence policy, nor the retroactive coverage typical of a claims made policy" (*Sparks, supra,* at page 332).

The Court reasoned that judicial intervention was necessary in dealing with insurance contracts "in order to prevent overreaching and injustice"(*id.,* page 338). The Court went on to say that it had a "special responsibility to prevent the marketing of policies that provide unrealistic and inadequate coverage" (*id.,* page 341). As a consequence, the Court concluded that the policy issued by St. Paul, which provided no retroactive coverage during the first year and limited retroactive coverage in subsequent policy terms, did not "objectively" meet the reasonable expectations of the insured or professional liability insurance. The Court went on to say that there was no evidence that the reduced coverage was bargained-for by way of a premium reduction. It was clearly suggested that had there been negotiations for the bargained for exchange of coverage, the Court may have been inclined to enforce the claims made policy as written by St. Paul Insurance Company in this case.

The importance of determining the validity of these policies is evident. Most lawyers' professional liability carriers have resisted efforts to clarify this issue. By allowing for a negotiated coverage, most insurance carriers eliminate any necessity for determining whether or not the limitations in coverage are reasonable and meet the ordinary expectations of an insured. As a consequence, the law governing claims made policies is still in the developmental stages, at least as it pertains to the application of the various forms.

One final example may be found in a case in which an insured attorney has reason to believe that a claim will be made against him or her during a policy term, but determines that no actual claim has been made. Therefore, no claim is reported. Thereafter, the insured attorney decides to secure legal malpractice insurance from a different carrier. More specifically, let's assume an insured has a policy with an effective date of January 1, 1988 and an expiration date of December 31, 1988. During this period of time the insured learns of an act, error, or omission which could reasonably be expected to be the basis of a claim. No claim, however, is filed by the client. The insured therefore determines not to place the malpractice insurance carrier on notice. On January 1, 1989 the insured secures legal malpractice insurance from another insurance carrier. If the client files a claim at this time (after January 1, 1989), the question becomes, Will the second carrier provide coverage? Presumably, the position of the second carrier would be that the insured attorney knew or had reason to know of the existence of this claim in 1988, prior to the inception date. As a consequence, when a claim is made against that attorney in 1989, the insurance carrier will decline coverage. When presented to the carrier which covered the insured for the calendar year 1988, that carrier will probably assert that the insured failed to give the carrier notice of a claim on a timely basis or during the policy term of the calendar year 1988. Looking at *Zuckerman* and *Sparks,* as well as all of the other cases decided in various jurisdictions, this situation would theoretically present a real dilemma: no malpractice coverage for this loss. Claims made policies need to be reconsidered, before it is too late. If we wait much longer, the inevitable result will be a substantial number of uninsured events for attorneys. This would directly impact the public; clients would face severe restrictions in the collection of judgments against attorneys. If the attorney is negligent, let there be broad-based insurance to cover the loss suffered by the victim.

THE INSURING AGREEMENT: WHAT IS COVERED

THE INSURING agreement is designed to set forth the specific purpose and intent of the insurance coverage which is available under the terms and conditions of the lawyers' malpractice insurance policy. Generally, it is said that one looks to exclusions in the policy to determine what is not covered. The corollary is that one must look to the insuring agreement, particularly under "coverage," to determine specifically what is covered by the lawyers' professional liability insurance policy. Typically, the language of the insurance agreement states that the insurance carrier will pay on behalf of the insured all sums which the insured shall become legally obligated to pay as damages as a result of claims first made against the insured during the policy period for acts, errors, or omissions of the insured in rendering or failing to render professional services for others in the insured's capacity as a lawyer. This general provision will vary substantially from insurance company to insurance company.

The more modern approach is to state a general purpose of coverage and incorporate a series of subsections relating to the coverage which is afforded. For example, many policies will state that the company will pay on behalf of the insured all sums "in excess of the deductible amount stated in the declarations." This effort by the insurance company is obviously designed to compel the insured attorney to come forward to pay his or her deductible amount prior to the insurance carrier's making any payments — either for expense or indemnity, as the case may be. Another example of an insurance carriers' effort at expanding the scope of the traditional coverage portion of the insuring agreement includes provisions such as identifying non-lawyer employees as being covered under the terms and conditions of the policy subject to certain conditions. At this point it is important to note that the coverage portion of the insuring agreement should not be read in isolation. Rather, one should read the definition section along with the declarations page which identifies the amount of coverage and the name of the insured. In many instances this section includes the application which may be attached to the policy and incorporated by reference.

I mentioned the hybrid claims made policy in prior sections. An examination of a hybrid claims made policy reveals that the coverage portion of the insuring agreement states that all claims have to be first made against the insured lawyer during the policy period and reported to the insurance company during the policy period. In addition, the act, error, or omission has to occur during the same policy period. Once again, these policies are subject to both state regulation and judicial scrutiny. There are many insurance companies that seek to restrict coverage in the insuring agreement by excluding prior acts, or what is commonly referred to as "retroactive coverage." We have examined *Zuckerman, Sparks,* and other cases which challenge the insurance carriers' exclusion of retroactive or prior acts in the absence of a bargained-for negotiation. By excluding this type of coverage, it would seem that the insurance carrier seeks to gain the benefit of an occurrence policy which would naturally exclude any prior act, error, or omission, yet at the same time gain the benefit of a claims made policy requiring a claim be made to the insured and reported to the company, both within the policy term. This aspect of the claims made policy is predicated generally upon the belief that the insured did not know or should not know of or foresee any circumstances which might be expected to be the basis of a claim being specifically disclosed and excluded from coverage of the claims made policy. The modern policy may now include a specific statement to that effect in the coverage portion. Alternatively, this specific provision relating to knowledge of prior acts may either be a condition to the policy or a specific exclusion.

The coverage portion of the insuring agreement should also clarify in what capacity the insured will be covered. Rarely will a policy limit the insured's activities to those as a "lawyer." Rather, the majority of insurance policies will include acts in which the insured attorney acts as a notary public. The capacity issue also arises when a claim is made arising out of the insured's conduct, let's say as a trustee in a bankruptcy proceeding. The capacity question arises whether or not that type of activity, namely, as a trustee, is indeed covered under the terms and conditions of the insuring agreement. Other conduct of attorneys acting, for example, in the capacity of an officer or director of a corporation may not be covered under the terms and conditions of the policy. The policy of insurance may specifically exclude coverage for acts arising out of the insured's capacity as an officer or director of a corporation. In fact, the modern application form may request such information be disclosed by the lawyer-applicant. A seasoned claims examiner of an insurance company will look for businesses created by insured attorneys who establish separate and distinct entities which are unrelated to the practice of law. Such entities include a title company as an adjunct service to an attorney's law office. If, in the event the attorney is sued for a claim arising out of conduct relating to the title company, there would be no basis of coverage under a carefully worded lawyer's professional insurance policy.

The issue of what constitutes damages is one which has been historically the subject of considerable debate in the insurance industry. In many cases there are complaints against lawyers which seek equitable relief by way of injunction, restraining order, and the like. The question arises whether or not this type of relief, namely, equitable relief, constitutes damage claims within the terms and conditions of the insuring agreement. In the body of the policy found in the "exclusions" portion there is generally an express exclusion for equitable relief. One may also find an exclusion specifically directed at fines or penalties. What effect does Federal Rule 11 have in invoking coverage of the policy of insurance? This is the rule which allows for sanctions against lawyers for certain conduct. Therefore, would a claim for abuse of process or malicious prosecution, if it were otherwise covered by the terms and conditions of the policy, be barred by the fact that the damages sought to be recovered would be in the form of either punitive damages or a penalty? The claim for abuse of process or malicious prosecution may not be covered acts. The conduct may involve intentional conduct, malicious acts, or other acts or activities which may be found excluded in the policy of insurance.

There is also a general statement in most insuring agreements that allows for coverage of persons for whom the insured is either legally responsible or for any non-lawyer employee generally arising out of those legal services rendered within the scope of the individual's employment. The scope of the coverage is best determined by referring to the definition section or to that section that defines the term "insured." To determine who is actually insured under the terms and conditions of the policy, one must examine first the insured as the term is defined in the policy. This must be done in conjunction with a review of the declarations page, application, endorsements, and other relevant provisions of the policy. With the mobility of today's law society, including the growth and dissolution of the mega-law firms, the policy section entitled "insured" has stirred a raging debate in the insurance industry. As a practical matter the persons insured under the terms and conditions of a legal malpractice insurance policy differ dramatically from company to company because of the specific language of each policy and its interpretation. Let's now analyze the general policy language which governs provisions of this type.

WHO ARE THE PERSONS INSURED?

THE NAME of the insured is identified in the declarations section of the policy. The name of the person to whom the policy is issued does not limit the individuals or entities that will be covered under the policy of insurance. One must look to the definition section in order to determine the meaning of the term "insured" within the context of the policy. Generally the insured will be those persons named in the declarations page — any lawyer, legal corporation, or partnership, along with any partner, officer, director, or employee of the firm. The debate surrounding the persons insured generally involves predecessor law firms or attorneys who were former partners, officers, or directors or employees of the firm while acting on behalf of the law firm. Many policies will now provide for specific coverage for those individuals who were members of a predecessor firm and may now be retired or have moved on or otherwise become associated with other law firms. It is in this context that questions arise. For example, which policy would have application when an insured attorney formerly covered under a professional liability policy of one firm leaves that firm and becomes a member, partner, or shareholder of another law firm?

There is a variety of circumstances which have not

been addressed by decisional law concerning who is covered and under what circumstances coverage actually exists. For example, many policies now provide for a non-lawyer to be covered, provided that the individual acts within the scope of duties performed on behalf of the firm. The "of counsel" arrangement, which is now commonplace in the law marketplace, has not been clearly defined by most lawyers' professional liability insurance policies. In many instances, "of counsel" will be covered provided that the "of counsel" is performing services on behalf of the named insured. The question becomes, in some cases, when is "of counsel" service considered service to the law firm? The uncertainty of coverage can be resolved by naming the "of counsel" as a named insured in the insurance policy.

Most professional liability policies provide coverage extending to the heirs, executors, assigns, or administrators of the insured in the event of incapacity, death, or bankruptcy. The most common dilemma created by these circumstances, from the point of view of a claims examiner of the insurance carrier, stems from the fact that the executor or administrator of the lawyer or law firm does not place the insurance carrier on notice of potential claims in a timely manner. More often than not, these matters are not reported to the insurance carrier within the policy term and, in most instances, this will defeat coverage when the claim is thereafter reported. In other words, there will be no insurance coverage for this loss.

DEFENSE AND SETTLEMENT
PROVISIONS OF INSURANCE

MOST LAWYERS' professional liability policies combine both defense and settlement sections despite the fact that they are unrelated. The provisions of the insurance policy regarding the insurers' obligation to defend a claim bears no relationship to the obligation of the insured to settle the claim with or without the insurer's consent. For the purposes of this discussion, the analysis of defense and settlement will be separate and subdivided within this section.

With respect to the defense of a claim, it is frequently said that the insurance carriers' duty to defend is broader than its duty to pay. Other interpretations of insurance policies focus on the theory that they are contracts of adhesion which in many instances are unenforceable as against public policy. Let's examine the section in most lawyers' professional liability policies which govern defense of lawsuits. Generally it is provided in this section of the policy that "with respect to insurance afforded by this policy," the company will be obligated to defend any claim against the insured even if the claims are groundless, false, or fraudulent. The company reserves the right or has the corresponding duty to make any investigation it deems appropriate. The issue of the company's duty to pay for an appeal may or may not be addressed under the terms and conditions of this particular section. Of interest to most lawyers is whether or not the insurance company is obligated to defend a claim filed in an administrative hearing. This includes an attorney's appearance before an ethics proceeding. The defense provisions of the insurance policy rarely address these issues.

There is also the question of the selection of defense counsel and how that may impact on the terms and conditions of this particular section, but this issue will be dealt with in later chapters. Judicial interpretation of the insurer's obligation has been the cause of considerable debate and has resulted in much state legislation in recent years. As a consequence of the impact upon both the client and lawyer, a separate section later in this book is devoted to a discussion of these issues. For the purpose of this section, however, suffice it to say that in making a determination as to whether or not the insurance carrier is obligated to provide a defense, the claims examiner or adjustor is obligated to go beyond the four corners of a complaint or statement and conduct an investigation to determine whether or not part or all of the allegations are covered by the policy of insurance. If any of the allegations are covered by the policy of insurance, the insurance company will be obligated to provide a defense in most jurisdictions.

Most lawyers' professional liability insurance policies have a provision that allows for settlement only with the written consent of the insured. A problem arises with what is often referred to as the "blackmail clause," wherein the insurance carrier reserves the right to serve notice on the insured that, if the insured should refuse settlement of the claim, the insured may then be responsible for any excess judgment, settlement, or award above which the carrier had agreed to settle. Even in the absence of such language, a carrier may hold an insured responsible in the event that the insured should refuse to consent to settle. The insured may also be told by the insurance carrier that he or she is liable for any claims expenses, which include counsel's fees incurred in the defense of the claim subsequent to the date that the insured refused to settle. Most of these arguments are predicated upon an insured's unreasonably withholding his or her consent to settlement. A determination as to whether or not the withholding of consent could be deemed unreasonable may not be determinable until such time as a jury verdict is returned. As a practical matter, therefore, an insurance carrier negotiating a settlement with a claimant negotiates the settlement subject to the insured's written consent. Many times, however, defense counsel, assigned by the insurance carrier, may be in a compromising situation by negotiating such a settlement. In one recent case, counsel was held liable for damages for negotiating a settlement over the insured's objection to such a settlement. (*Lieberman v. Employers Insurance of Wausau*, 84 N.J. 325 [1980]).

Generally within this section there is a limitation of liability by the insurance carrier. The insurance company will seek to limit its liability to defend any claim or pay any judgment. Once the insurance company has paid its policy limits for defense or indemnity or both, the insured then has responsibility to pay all additional monies. This is true only when the policy of insurance is one that reduces the amount of coverage available by both defense costs and indemnity payments. This appears to be the most commonly used policy of insurance in recent years. A real question arises when the insurance carrier, as a practical matter, attempts to tender the defense back to the insured after its limits of liability have been exhausted. This presents complex problems for both the insurance carrier and for the insured attorney in terms of a transition of a file. This may even raise questions as to the insurer's authority to withdraw from the defense of a claim. Other dilemmas concern the defense attorney's application to withdraw from the defense of a claim based solely on the insurance carrier's having exhausted its limits of liability. This would certainly have an impact on the administration of justice when insurance carriers and defense attorneys assigned by those insurance carriers seek to withdraw from the defense of a claim after a considerable amount of litigation has transpired. Therefore, this procedure raises a number of legal issues that need to be addressed by each individual jurisdiction.

EXCLUSIONS: WHAT IS NOT COVERED

IF ONE looks to the coverage portion of the insuring agreement to determine the extent of insurance coverage afforded by the policy, one must look to the exclusion portion of the policy to determine what is not covered. Lawyers' professional liability insurance will vary from carrier to carrier. The fact remains that there are some universal aspects of conduct which are excluded from insurance policies. Much of the method and manner in which insurance carriers exclude coverage is a function of philosophy and design. However, all agree that false, fraudulent, criminal, dishonest, or maliciously deliberate acts should be excluded from coverage. Most policies will not include coverage for acts of attorneys involved in securities matters absent an endorsement to the contrary. If a claim is made against the insured attorney for conduct arising out of a business enterprise which is not the named insured in the policy, any resulting obligation under the policy will be disclaimed. Where punitive damages are uninsurable by law, the policy will generally specify an exclusion to that effect. Other conduct, including acts arising out of discrimination by the insured, may be excluded as well. One must carefully examine the language of the entire policy to determine what, if any, coverage is available for bodily injury, personal injury, and other causes of actions. The exclusion portion of the policy may be the appropriate place to first examine and determine whether or not there are specific exclusions which concern these issues. Prior acts may also be excluded if the insured knew or could have reasonably foreseen that his or her conduct would give rise to a claim. There are a variety of other exclusions which may be included in any lawyers' professional liability policy.

A lawyer who has options in selecting a professional liability insurance carrier should examine these provisions prior to the submission of any application form. This procedure is rarely followed. Most attorneys are generally unaware of coverage and the applicable exclusions until a claim is first made against them. I recommend that a sample policy be reviewed prior to submitting an application for the policy of insurance.

A recent phenomenon has occurred in lawyers' professional liability litigation. In most instances, the complaint against an attorney will allege both covered and non-covered grounds. This area is examined in detail from the perspective of the victim or former client, the insured attorney, and the insurance carrier in later chapters.

MISCELLANEOUS PROVISIONS

MOST LAWYERS' professional liability insurance has boilerplate provisions which include as a prerequisite to coverage that the insured file a notice of a claim and all pertinent information about the claim as soon as practicable. Most policies also require the reporting of a lawsuit immediately after service is made upon an insured attorney. These notice conditions are separate and apart from the notice requirements within the policy term as discussed in the previous section dealing with claims made versus occurrence policies.

Most professional liability insurance policies also include limits of liability which set forth the company's financial responsibility in connection with overall amounts of coverage. The policy's "territory" provisions are other aspects of the policy which refer to whether the insurance will have application outside a particular state or territory. "Extended reporting" endorsements, or options to extend the reporting period, are important to consider, particularly when an attorney is either leaving the practice of law or anticipates having a hiatus of coverage. As an observation, most provisions allowing for an option of extended reporting endorsement allow for an insured to report a claim beyond the ordinary discovery period for conduct occurring prior to the termination of the insured's private practice and provided further that there is no other insurance applicable to such coverage. The payment of premium for this coverage is generally a proportional amount depending upon the extended reporting period.

Another provision of interest to be found in most policies, concerns "other insurance." Prior insurance, concurrent insurance, or insurance which is purchased in the future may have application to a claim being made against an attorney. In many instances the other insurance provision will state that the loss will be prorated based upon the limits set for both policies or, in the alternative, the limits of the applicable coverage will be in excess of any other insurance that may be applicable. In many instances, the courts determine the application of the various policies either by public policy considerations or by consideration of the premium paid and the insurance afforded under the respective policies.

The entire insurance process, including the policy and its application to legal malpractice, is an area known to a select few. When ambiguities in policy interpretation and coverage arise, the courts generally resolve in favor of the insured. On the other hand, every effort is made by the insurance industry to avoid coverage. As a consequence, experts are needed to assist either claimants or an insured when dealing with insurance carriers who seek to avoid coverage, even when the basis of such avoidance is questionable. ≡

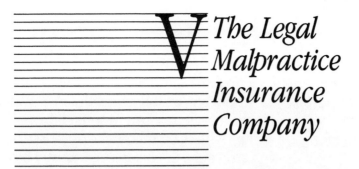

V The Legal Malpractice Insurance Company

THE INSURANCE COMPANY & THE LEGAL MALPRACTICE CRISIS

CONTROVERSY SUR-ROUNDS the origin and causes of the legal malpractice insurance crisis. Certainly the insurance industry must accept a large measure of responsibility for the present malpractice crisis. While there are, of course, a variety of factors which have contributed to the explosion of legal malpractice litigation, the legal malpractice insurance industry has been in the unique position of having firsthand insight into this crisis as has developed over time into its present form. The legal malpractice insurance industry has been called upon in a variety of ways to respond to this challenge; and, even today, the legal malpractice insurance industry could have a significant impact in dealing with this crisis.

By and large, however, the legal malpractice insurance industry has failed to respond to this challenge. It has relied upon traditional insurance industry practices instead of focusing its attention on the legal malpractice crisis. Regrettably, the legal malpractice insurance industry has confronted the crises by choosing to rely upon a steady spiralling cost of legal malpractice insurance. It is content to rely upon these rate increases to build its premium coffers. Instead of dealing with the crisis and providing creative solutions to the problems, it has opted for a hands-off approach to the legal profession in its efforts to main-

71

tain constant premium cash flow. The industry ignores the long term effects of its actions.

The purpose of insurance in the original sense was simply a pooling of resources in an effort to spread the risk of loss amongst a group with a common classification of risks or liabilities. Unfortunately, the insurance industry has moved away from its common experience and has instead looked to a bottom-line orientation of profit without consideration to its original purpose and function. When we speak of the traditional insurance industry, we are talking in terms of a capital stock traditional insurance carrier.

There are other types of insurance carriers organized for various different purposes. One such is comprised of the mutual insurance companies which are theoretically owned by their insureds. These groups are not included in the group which is usually referred to as the traditional insurance carriers. Rather, the standard stock company and, occasionally, the mutual company are responsible for writing the majority of legal malpractice insurance. There are captive insurance groups that dominate certain areas and are growing at an increasing rate. A later section of this book deals with the function and use of a captive insurance group in all facets of lawyers' professional liability insurance. The focus of attention of this particular chapter, however, is directed at the standard legal malpractice insurance company.

In its very basic form, the standard stock insurance company collects premiums. The insured receives no benefit or dividends from any earnings of the company. By the same token, the insured pays no additional premium for any losses that may be incurred during a policy period. The claims made policy, however, enables the pure stock insurance company to charge additional premium for any losses immediately succeeding the calendar year. The stock insurance carrier invests a premium and earns additional money from that premium. At the end of the year, the stockholders may or may not be entitled to a dividend. The mutual insurance company is theoretically owned by its policyholders or its insureds. There are various different types of mutual insurance companies, but essentially they are designed strictly for the policyholder and are managed by the policyholder's management groups. The captive insurance groups and the private insurance carriers are specifically designed for a limited purpose in the insurance market.

In the early years, legal malpractice insurance carriers writing lawyers' professional liability insurance enjoyed an almost risk-free environment. Rarely, if ever, were claims made against lawyers. At that time, the insurance industry wrote lawyers' professional liability policies which collected premiums resulting in a highly profitable program. Several changes have occurred that have dramatically altered the state of affairs in the legal malpractice insurance, at least from the malpractice carriers' perspective. Most significantly, society has become more more litigious. Clients have also become more sophisticated in recognizing the errors lawyers make in handling their matters. With the increase in the number of lawyers, young members of the Bar have been looking for new ways to expand a practice —they have sought legitimate, new causes of action. For insurance carriers, there has also been the problem of unlimited "tail" coverage from the occurrence policy, which provided no real basis for accurate predictability of future premiums. As a consequence, as noted in preceding chapters, the claims made policy developed. Even with this abundance of signs indicating the development of a crisis, the insurance industry has steadfastly refused to respond. It has taken no action whatsoever to anticipate the development of this crisis. Coincident with the development of this crisis there has also been a dramatic drop in interest rates. Poor investment by the insurance carriers resulted in the loss of substantial premium dollars. At the same time, attorneys have learned that they have to act as both lawyer and businessman or businesswoman in order to survive among the modern day economic realities. All of these factors combined to create the real crisis in lawyers' malpractice insurance, a crisis the traditional insurance industry has chosen to ignore.

As we will see, the insurance industry has resisted all efforts toward change. It has tolerated no innovative responses to this crisis; its only response has been to raise rates. The established industry also has begun to lose significant amounts of business to the captive insurance groups. It has also withdrawn from writing certain lines of business in certain jurisdictions in an effort to raise the rates of insurance. The claims personnel, as we shall see, have been unprepared to meet this crisis. They are ill-equipped in terms of both education and experience. As a consequence, there has been sloppy claims handling, and the underwriting departments have panicked. While this may seem to be an oversimplification of a dramatic financial crisis, it is nevertheless a simple description of what has taken place in the insurance industry marketplace. As a consequence, we have seen increasing numbers of captive insurance groups which present very real alternatives and competition to the traditional insurance industry. There is no doubt that the captive insurance industry will be responsible for writing a substantial premium dollar volume in direct competition with the traditional insurance carriers in the future.

Let's now examine the insurance carrier as an institution and specifically examine each department in relation to the legal malpractice insurance crisis.

THE UNDERWRITING DEPARTMENT: THE PROFIT CENTER

THE UNDERWRITING department is the salesperson of the legal malpractice insurance industry. It is indeed the profit center. While actuarial, investment, real estate, and all other departments of the insurance company have a hand in profitability, it is underwriting that is the bottom-line motivator in the traditional insurance industry. I have often questioned why the claims department should not be merged with the underwriting department, for reasons that will become clear in the following sections. One only has to visit the underwriting department to see firsthand the importance that the traditional legal malpractice insurance industry places on underwriting. It is apparent from the physical layout of each underwriting department that it is afforded full deference. Generally, underwriting has lavish offices; unlike its stepsister, the claims department, the underwriting department enjoys the full fruits of its labor.

The underwriting function basically consists of writing insurance business. It is primarily responsible for the negotiation of policies and for setting rates. These rates may initially be determined in the actuarial department but it is the underwriting department that negotiates these rates with the insureds. When I say "with the insureds," I mean as it applies in legal malpractice insurance, for either professional associations or on a statewide basis. Underwriting, traditionally, is not chargeable with the responsibility of forecasting what losses may occur. In the real world, however, it is underwriting that is responsible for all aspects of profitability. Underwriting also determines whether or not a particular risk will be insured by the insurance carrier. It is therefore responsible for the selection of risks. For that reason, when an application for lawyers' professional liability coverage is submitted, it is underwriting which ultimately determines whether or not the risk will be accepted. It is underwriting that is also responsible for negotiations concerning specific coverages that may or may not be available in a legal malpractice insurance policy, including a determination as to what deductible will be applicable to the policy. While outside the scope of this, it should be noted that underwriting also is involved in the reinsurance market in determining what portion of the risk, if any, will be retained and what type of reinsurance will be negotiated for a given program.

The real dilemma arises when, as we have seen in recent years, the insurance investment premium dollar is earning very little and the losses have risen to a dramatic level in lawyers' professional liability. As a consequence, the underwriter is under intense pressure to increase rates to cover the losses. Traditionally, most insurance carriers have looked to profit from investment. Today insurance executives are looking to the underwriting department to provide a profit, which would mean that their loss ratio would automatically give underwriting a profit without consideration to any investment income which may be derived. As a consequence of the pressure being applied to the underwriting department, it becomes increasingly more obvious that the underwriters must forecast losses with more predictability and, to do so, they naturally look to the claims department for guidance. Unfortunately, the roles of underwriting and claims within a traditional legal malpractice insurance carrier have been adversarial in nature. Each department competes with the other in an effort to place fault or blame for the profitability crisis on the other's performance. For example, underwriting takes the position that the claims department did not properly evaluate the cases to accurately predict the loss structure. Claims, on the other hand, says that underwriting did not properly price the program with adequate rates and reserves to insure profitability. As a consequence of these competing views, no creative approaches have been structured to eliminate the malpractice crisis. Instead these groups continue to compete and place fault with one another to the detriment of not only the insurance industry as a whole but, more important, to its insureds and ultimate claimants, the real victims of the legal malpractice crisis. This competition within prevents sound judgment in the operation of the insurance company.

By way of example, let me illustrate one of my own experiences with this self-destructive approach on the part of the insurance carrier. When I was serving as national claims manager, I was visited by a representative of the president of one division. This division was responsible for writing most of the lawyers' professional liability insurance coverages. I was asked to name specific areas in which we could recoup losses common among traditional insurance companies. The question of deductibles was raised during the course of the conversation. I responded by indicating that no effort had been made whatsoever to collect deductibles from insureds. Let me explain in some detail this entire mechanism and process. When an insured has a deductible of $1,000, for example, and the company has a loss on the policy of $10,000, the question arises as to the method for collecting that $1,000 payment. Most insurance carriers would probably be obligated to pay the $10,000 payment to a claimant and make an effort at collecting the $1,000 payment directly from its insured. An alternative method would be to have the insurance carrier pay $9,000 and request the insured pay $1,000, and then together present the $10,000 payment to the claimant. What was happening in the miscellaneous professional liability division was that payments were made to the claimants without any effort at collecting the deductibles from the insureds.

I was certain that substantial sums of money could be collected by recovering deductibles which had not been paid. As a result of my candid appraisal of the circumstances which cost the carrier millions of dollars, which in turn cost the consumer millions of dollars, my position with the carrier as national professional liability claims manager was in jeopardy. The head of worldwide claims also served on the board of directors of this particular insurance carrier. He actually threatened me with termination for disclosing information to a representative of the president of the division, who happened to be an employee of the underwriting department. The reasoning was simple. Rather than identify the problem and implement procedures to correct the problem, it was far better to cover up the facts in order to avoid any suggestion that the traditional method of doing things was ineffective. In other words, persons in positions of authority guarded the traditional methods of doing business at the cost of millions and millions of dollars. This is just one example of underwriting's inability to deal with the crisis.

There are countless programs that should be initiated to combat this crisis in legal malpractice, but with the lack of cooperation between the two divisions, there will be no creative solutions implemented by the traditional insurance carrier. Each is unwilling to go to the chief executive officer to suggest procedures to deal with this crisis. As a consequence, insurance carriers risk greater losses in the years to come. In looking at the claims department, it is obvious that its present structure is outdated and inadequate. However, it remains a dinosaur because of the apathy and traditional mechanisms still in place within many legal malpractice insurance carriers.

THE CLAIMS DEPARTMENT: THE UNPROFIT CENTER

WHILE UNDERWRITING clearly represents the profit center of the traditional legal malpractice insurance carrier, the claims department is considered the "unprofit center." As we approach the 1990's, there is no legitimate reason for the claims department to be viewed as the unprofit center. Instead, it is here that many of the very profitable reforms may be instituted to correct this legal malpractice crisis. Let's examine the claims department and its structure in order to better understand its development and current daily function.

Like the underwriting center, the claims department has not been equipped to handle the emerging crisis in legal liability insurance.

In theory, the claims department's function is to receive, analyze, review, and where appropriate, settle claims that are submitted to an insurance company. This department is is also responsible for monitoring defense counsel and determining whether or not the costs incurred in connection with a defense of a claim are appropriate. In addition, the claims department should have the decision-making ability to determine which law firms will be representing both the insurance company and the individual insured attorneys who are the targets of legal malpractice lawsuits. In theory, there is no reason why the claims department should not also advise as to the circumstances under which certain risks should be written by the underwriting department. In reality, the claims department operates in a much different manner. The antiquated methods used by the traditional insurance carrier in handling lawyers' professional liability claims are partially at fault for inhibiting the development of new methods for dealing with the legal malpractice crisis.

In addition, as the national claims manager of professional liability claims, it didn't take me long to learn that the hierarchy of the claims administration would consistently be blamed for the losses incurred during the legal malpractice crisis and insurance crunch. In part, the claims department was indeed responsible; the greatest fault of the claims department was its failure to come forward and persuade the chief executive officer that a dramatic change was necessary. Instead, it covered up its failures and camouflaged the real problem by shifting the focus of attention from the substance of the problem to its form. For example, the claims department would have a constant employee turnover. This included executive personnel right down through the claims examiner or adjustors who handled the claims. Defense counsel, independent adjustors, and all personnel associated with the claims department could lose their jobs for suggesting reforms. Every effort made at changing or improving the system was viewed as heresy. I recall making many suggestions for necessary changes. In fact, even after I left the full-time employment of the insurance industry, I wrote to many chief executive officers hoping to influence the way claims were handled in lawyers' professional liability and their professional liability lines. The changes I proposed after I left the insurance industry were met with more hostility and aggression than ever. Clearly, those responsible for correcting gross inefficiencies were not interested in doing their jobs creatively. What we are really dealing with is a crisis caused by people who had the authority to make changes, but would not admit that the system needed to changed. Instead they have viewed each and every suggestion of improvement as a direct threat to their individual positions. As a consequence, the system has perpetuated itself. Even today it is, for the most part, still unchanged. Let's now examine the hierarchy of claims personnel and see how each level functions in its respective role during this insurance crisis.

THE HIERARCHY OF THE CLAIMS DEPARTMENT

AT THE very top of each major traditional insurance carrier hierarchy is an individual who has overall responsibility for the entire claims department. In my experience, this individual sat on the board of directors and enjoyed at that time the title of head of worldwide claims. This person reported directly to the chief executive officer of the corporation. All claims personnel reported through the proper lines to this one individual. In one particular case, this man also held the title of senior vice president of the group of companies which formed the component parts of the one parent company. In this role, the individual was responsible for most of the major decision making. He was also the person to whom a president of a division, most often the one who headed the underwriting department of that division, reported to discuss the overall operation of the claims department and its impact on the profitability of lawyers' professional liability.

While this structure has changed to some extent, one important element remains intact in most traditional lawyers' professional liability companies. This is the separation between underwriting and claims. As noted, this lack of unity between two closely related departments has been largely responsible for failing to resolve the problems with implementing reforms concerning the insurance crisis in lawyers' professional liability. From my own experience, there is no question that this structure with this individual as head is responsible more than anything else for the stagnation of the claims process. It has not only short-circuited progress, but still continues to do so. The system sabotages creative effort. Loyalty to the existing structure translates into catastrophic losses to both the consumer and the insured group of lawyers.

The company, of course, has suffered during this period and it has only been through the incredible acceleration of premium dollars through the underwriting department's efforts that these programs have been saved. I have no doubt that this structural problem is prevalent throughout the industry.

Generally, most claims which exceed one million dollars in exposure are reviewed directly by the head of claims, either through one of his direct representatives or by himself. As we will see, most of the personnel at this high level of management were at one time themselves claims examiners and herein lies the greatest problem confronting the lawyers' professional liability claims department. Once an examiner demonstrates any level of competence in the area of being a technician in lawyers' professional liability claims, he or she is immediately promoted and elevated through the claims hierarchy. As indicated, it is not uncommon that the chief of claims was once a claims examiner. The difficulty here is that nothing indicates that the promoted individual, who now heads overall supervision and jurisdiction of all claims, has any management skills. Generally, the "Peter Principle" is commonly found in the operation of a lawyers' professional liability claims department. Unfortunately, the individual who demonstrates the technical ability, and is raced upward through the hierarchy of responsibility, is the person that often doesn't have the necessary requisite management skills to innovate and create solutions to the problems mentioned. The highest level of management in lawyers' profession is often made up of skilled technicians.

Similarly, the vice president and assistant vice presidents of claims are those persons who have demonstrated a high degree of efficiency in performing tasks as technicians. Because of the overall nationwide shortage of qualified lawyers' professional liability claims personnel, these individuals are automatically promoted. In my own experience, my climb from examiner in professional liability claims to manager of a nationwide professional liability claims department took a year-and-a-half. This time frame seems to be common throughout the traditional lawyers' professional liability industry.

The manager of claims is responsible for recruiting, hiring, and training claims personnel. Very little or no effort is made toward the specialization of the manager, either in human relations or in the application of technical guidance for the individual examiners or adjustors. Generally, the manager of professional liability claims has spent a little time as an examiner and then as a supervisor of professional liability and has demonstrated some skill in those respective tasks. As a consequence of his or her exposure through the presentation of high exposure claims, he or she develops greater visibility. This is the individual that generally becomes manager of professional liability claims. This person may or may not be an attorney. In fact, in many cases, the individuals composing the hierarchy may not be trained in the law. In most instances the members of the hierarchy are simply experienced, seasoned claims personnel who have risen through the ranks. The manager of professional liability claims may have as many as thirty claims people for whom he or she is responsible. In addition, there may be an administrative staff which directly reports to the same manager. A claims department may also be broken down in terms of either lawyer or accountant-related claims, or it may segregate the individual claims according to the purposes of internal operations. In other words, there may be one department specifically designed for lawyers' professional liability claims.

Next in the hierarchy is the supervisor or superintendent of claims. This individual generally has a small group of claims personnel — anywhere from five to fifteen people — reporting directly to him or her. Theoretically, the supervisor has greater responsibility and authority to settle claims. In addition, the supervisor oversees the operation of the claims examiners. While, in theory, the supervisor should review the work of each individual examiner, this rarely ever occurs. Usually the supervisor maintains a diary of high exposure cases and this occupies most of his or her time. He or she must fill the job function of manning a desk in the absence of an examiner. Since there is a crucial shortage of qualified, legally trained, professional liability claims examiners, this responsibility can be very time, consuming for supervisors. Supervisors frequently must abandon their supervisory roles and serve as substitute claims examiners.

As we follow the hierarchy of claims to the bottom, we last find the claims examiner or adjustor. While this is a grass-roots level position, it is probably the most significant in all of the claims hierarchy positions. However, as we will see later in this chapter, there is very little emphasis placed on the importance of the claims personnel at this level. Generally, these people are neither well trained nor well paid. Many are terribly ill-equipped to deal with the many complex facets of the lawyers' professional liability crisis. For example, my first day on the job, I was instructed to read the policies which had been written. By the second day I was already handling lawyers' professional liability claims! While the training methods may have improved since my days as a beginning examiner, they still do not meet other minimum commercial standards. For example, when videotaping actual sessions for starting examiners was suggested to management, it was casually dismissed.

Therefore, the claims examiner who may have been the adjustor for automobile liability claims just weeks before may now be responsible for a first notice suit resulting in binding the company to coverage and settlement or defense in the millions of dollars. This individual may or may not be an attorney and may or may not be ready for such an assignment. Thus, it is here where my biggest concerns lie, since this is where there is the most significant impact in the overall handling of lawyers' professional liability claims and this is where there is a dramatic loss of valuable coverage decisions. Moreover, it is here where the claims are handled on an irregular basis. The examiner has the greatest impact on this overall process of lawyers' professional liability claims, but at the present time is the least equipped to deal with this crisis.

It is at the bottom of this hierarchy that my concerns lie. Why? Because it is here where losses are out of control.

RECEIPT & REVIEW OF FIRST NOTICE REPORTS

IN MOST cases, lawyers' professional liability insurance policies require that the insured attorney place his or her legal malpractice insurance carrier on notice of a claim as soon as practicable. All insurance policies require that the insured forward all summonses and complaints when they are served upon the insured attorney by a sheriff or other authorized agents. All insured attorneys are generally obligated to provide copies of the notice, together with copies of the summons or complaint and other information pertaining to the claim, directly to the managing general agent or to the claims department of the insurance carrier. This is referred to as the "notice requirement." Unfortunately, confusion generally reigns in this process. The insured is rarely, if ever, specifically instructed regarding the method and manner of the reporting process. To add to this confusion, insurance carriers seldom set up a predictable mechanism for the receipt and review of the first notice reports. Since many of the first notice reports are lawsuits requiring the defendant to respond or answer the complaint within a short duration of time, this process is crucial. Regrettably, the carrier is generally ill-equipped to deal with the sheer number of lawsuits which are reported on a first notice basis.

As a practical matter, the first notice reports are received by a clerk who then presents these claims to the claims manager. In theory, the claims manager reviews each and every claim to determine coverage issues or highlight certain aspects of the complaint for examination by the claims examiner. In many instances, the claims manager delegates this function to other claims personnel. In the real world, this process takes place so quickly that little or no attention is actually paid any substantive review of claims being made.

Because of the volume of new claims being submitted,

as well as the complexity of claims arising out of the lawyers' professional liability, the first notice function of the review and analysis is usually placed upon the shoulders of the claims examiner. This individual may or may not be an attorney, depending upon which insurance carrier is involved in defending the claim. The immediate function of the claims examiner is to read the complaint. The insured attorney usually provides only a summons and complaint at this early stage. Therefore, the claims examiner is responsible for contacting the insured's attorney and the attorney for the claimant to obtain the facts and circumstances surrounding the complaint. As I'll explain in later sections, the examiner is also chargeable with determining whether or not there is insurance coverage for the loss. In addition, the claims examiner must decide whether or not an independent investigator should be appointed, and as we will see in a later section, the claims examiner is responsible for the selection of defense counsel. Ideally, the claims examiner has available all the information essential for making an objective, accurate evaluation of the claim at this critical stage. However, this is rarely the case. Generally, the claims examiner doesn't have this information. As a consequence of not being fully informed, much time, money, and effort is lost at this early stage. Little effort is made at this time to settle claims.

The examiner or claims adjustor who is reviewing the claim on a first notice basis must look beyond what is commonly referred to as the "four corners of the complaint." This aspect is examined in some detail later. Setting aside for the moment the issue of insurance coverage, the claims adjustor or examiner must determine what the response will be to the notice of claim. Will the examiner attempt to settle the claim directly with the claimant's attorney? Will the examiner assign the matter to counsel for defense? Or, will the examiner undertake an investigation into the matter and seek to reserve its rights? What position will the insurance company take with respect to coverage issues? There are a number of issues which must be addressed at this posture of the claims process. In most instances, the claims examiner has insufficient evidence to make a comprehensive or very informed evaluation about the future course of the claim. As a consequence, the claims adjustor or examiner must rely upon outside factors to assist in the evaluation of the claim. It is at this point that the insured has the greatest input in terms of evaluation of the claim. Since most of the claims are met with denial, it is unlikely that the insured attorney will be cooperative in providing objective information. Outside counsel, as is pointed out in a later chapter, may have a conflict in the initial investigative stages, particularly when the issue of coverage is in dispute. It seems, therefore, that the only appropriate response is the assignment of a permanent outside investigator or claims adjustor who is retained solely to perform tasks on behalf of the insurance carrier. The investigator who is assigned by the carrier for the exclusive purpose of investigating coverage issues must be distinguished from the investigator who is assigned to investigate the defense of the facts in anticipation of settlement or defense of the claim. However, as a practical matter, no such distinctions exist at the present time. Most investigators or claims adjustors currently handling lawyers' professional liability claims are overburdened, ill-equipped, or inept at investigating claims of any magnitude.

I recommend that a highly skilled specialized staff of claims adjustors be trained for outside work. These people would determine either coverage issues or liability aspects of the case, depending upon their exclusive orientation. I believe that highly specialized experts are required to handle these matters since the greatest impact on any given claim may be realized right at these early stages. Unfortunately, it is here where current claims are met with the greatest ineptitude.

The receipt and review of first notice reports includes a process which is commonly referred to as "reserving a claim." Basically, a reserve placed on a file is meant to be an amount of money sufficient for anticipated expenditures in the defense of the claim, as well as for ultimate indemnity payments that will be made in connection with that claim. By law, a reserve must be set on each and every claim. In different states, the insurance department responsible for the regulation of insurance companies mandates certain procedures to insure that the insurance company remains solvent. The best way to verify the solvency of a particular insurance carrier is to simply look at the annual reserves to make certain that the carrier has sufficient capital on hand to make all anticipated payments for claims and expenses. Unfortunately, a real dilemma arises in lawyers' professional liability when the claims examiner or adjustor reviews a claim at its very early stages and has insufficient information to form an objective evaluation concerning the amount the reserve should be. As a consequence, many of these claims have inadequate reserves. In fact, one of the major causes of the developing insurance crisis in professional liability coverages has arisen from the inadequacies of the reserves. Simply stated, the carriers are not prepared for the losses sustained in insuring these various programs. Losses come in each year in excess of what was anticipated. Since the rates have already been established for the subsequent year, the insurance carrier is unable to recoup its losses. That fact, coupled with the lowering of interest rates and loss of the investment dollar, means that the insurance carriers are in a crisis situation regarding all lines of professional liability, especially lawyers' professional liability insurance.

As a result of the high volume of claims, the claims examiner or adjustor has little time to review the adequacies of the reserves as the case progresses during litigation. In fact, by making it an impossible task to present a reserve change, the insurance carrier ensures that the examiner will not make any alterations or modifications. The examiner is required to complete enormous paperwork and make it letter perfect. The examiner is then subjected to a grueling session of cross-examination to determine whether or not the reserve was adequate on his or her particular claim file. This not only discourages the examiner from making the appropriate modifications but it makes it impossible time-wise. The emphasis is clearly on form and not substance.

As the claim progresses, the examiner has little or no time to make any other evaluation of the value of the claim file. Often, defense counsel adds to the problems by failing to report to the claims examiner on a regular basis. The examiner, because of the sheer volume of cases, is no longer monitoring counsel, but rather has abandoned the claims functions directly to defense counsel. With defense counsel, who in many instances is not responsive to prompt and efficient claims handling, the claims oversight process simply becomes stale. The case is now set for trial. Trial counsel invariably calls the claims adjustor and indicates that the case has taken a dramatic turn for the worse and needs a substantial sum of money to settle the claim. It is obviously in the interests of defense counsel to continue the litigation. Settlements are not favored. The more work defense counsel has, the more profitable the handling of lawyers' professional liability becomes for that attorney or his or her law firm. By the time the defense counsel reports the situation to the claims examiner, the examiner has other concerns. By this time the damage has been done. The examiner will now be concerned with having to avoid presenting the case to his or her superiors for fear that he or she will be chastised for allowing the case to go without supervision. The examiner has two choices. One is to ignore the claimant and allow the case to go to verdict. The second is to report that defense counsel did not keep the claims examiner informed. Neither option is obviously helpful to the process. Incredibly, there are a substantial number of cases that actually go to trial without the knowledge or approval of the claims examiner. Verdicts are rendered in the millions of dollars without any supervision by the claims person. Let me share with you an experience which I had, to give you some indication of how claims are mismanaged.

When I first was hired as an examiner in the lawyers' and accountants' malpractice unit, I was assigned more than 600 claims. While the numbers on my assignment sheet did not reflect that high figure, it later turned out that I was actually responsible for handling each and every one of those 600-plus claims. In an effort to reduce my claim load, I wrote to defense counsel and asked defense counsel to provide written detail concerning every effort made at settlement of those claims within the past twelve months. Within a very short period of time, I received approximately 150 telephone calls from defense counsel requesting authority to settle cases that had miraculously moved to a settlement posture in a matter of days after receipt of my letter. To further evidence this chaotic situation, a newspaper reported an incident involving a former employee of an insurance adjustment company who initially had jurisdiction over the handling of these claims. It is alleged that there were circus-like conditions that led to a mail disposal party in which letters from attorneys and vendors were discarded. This is not unusual. Our problem wasn't so much discarding of mail as it was that it could not be matched with a particular file. This chaos continued for months on end without any relief. Upper managers had convinced themselves that there was no real problem. They refused to deal with the crisis.

The process of reserving a claim is significant in that without adequate reserve on a claim file, a claim cannot be settled. Unless the examiner who has authority to settle a claim at the very first stages secures adequate authority for the higher exposure claims, there will be no settlement of the claim. There are no typical reserve levels for the respective examiners or adjustors, but let's say that a first line adjustor has authority to make settlements up to $10,000. His or her supervisor has authority, up to let's say, $50,000. The manager of the unit has authority up to $100,000. The assistant vice president has authority up to $150,000 to $200,000 and the vice president may have authority up to $500,000 to $1,000,000. The numbers are relatively insignificant. What is important is the fact that there must be a structured process for securing higher level authority. Without that process being originated by an entry level examiner, the settlement process becomes much more difficult.

What happens now when we are presented with a notice of a potential claim, instead of an actual claim? In reality, when an attorney fulfills the intent of the insurance policy by providing the insurance carrier with a notice of a potential claim, the letter of notice is commonly met with a standard form response. The insurance carrier will generally take the position that, since no claim is made at the present time, there is no need to take any further action in connection with the handling of the matter. In reality, the insurance carrier may well indeed be waiving its rights and may be forever barred from denying coverage at a later date. We will examine those issues in greater detail in later sections. For now, suffice it to say that most letters of a potential claim get no response. There is a minimum reserve set on the potential claim and then the file is closed without further activity. As a consequence of this irresponsible claims handling, the claims department fails to notify underwriting of the potential presentation of a future substantial claim. Once again, this results in the claims department being unable to properly set the rate structure for the coming years. At this posture, the potential claim should be properly investigated and a decision should be made

concerning whether or not efforts should be made at negotiating the claim directly with the claimant. It is also at this
point that some ethical issues should be raised about
whether or not the insured attorney is obligated to bring
this matter to the attention of his or her client. I have consistently recommended that the attorney follow the guidance of the rules of professional conduct and notify the
client that a potential claim is being made. In every
instance, I will advise that the attorney ignore the provision
of the insurance policy that prohibits an informative, candid
response to the client. I recommend this action because it
is the only appropriate response. The attorney owes a duty
of fidelity to the client. Any compromise of that duty may
place the attorney's license to practice law in jeopardy. The
insurance companies, on the other hand, have traditionally
taken the position that if you ignore the claim, it may go
away. It is that very type of response which has compounded today's malpractice crisis. ≡

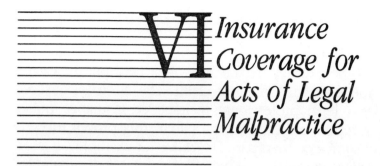

VI Insurance Coverage for Acts of Legal Malpractice

FIRST NOTICE REVIEW OF COVERAGE

GENERALLY, AN insured attorney forwards to his or her legal malpractice carrier or any of its authorized agents three types of notices. These include a claim letter from a client or an attorney representing the client, advising of a notice of a claim; a summons and complaint received by the attorney; or a letter by the insured attorney to his or her insurance carrier advising of the potential claim. Occasionally, there are third persons or attorneys representing former clients who send letters to the insured attorney's malpractice carrier as a direct means of notification. To limit this discussion, we shall deal only with the three methods of notification of a claim mentioned above for the purposes of reviewing coverages. In addition we shall assume that the insured in all instances forwards a claim directly to the legal malpractice insurance carrier or to one of its authorized agents. Problems often arise when a third person other than the insured reports the claim. In this type of situation, there may be some questions concerning the insured's obligation to report a claim as soon as practicable under the conditions of the policy. There also may be other issues raised in connection with this method of notification.

In the first instance, an insured may forward a letter of what we will describe as a potential claim. Within the tech-

93

nical definition of the policy, no claim has been made against the attorney. This letter will at least put the carrier on notice of the potential claim. The attorneys insured under a legal professional malpractice insurance policy rarely report potential items. Often, this proves to be a serious error on their part. Let's take, for example, an attorney whose complaint on behalf of a client is dismissed for failure to answer interrogatories. For purposes of this discussion, it is assumed that the failure to answer interrogatories on a timely basis was due to the lawyer's negligence and not a consequence of the client's misconduct.

While in most jurisdictions a complaint of that type may be restored by a pro forma application, the services rendered by the attorney are certainly suspect under the circumstances. This may give rise to a claim at some later date. In a case like this, the attorney should forward a letter to his or her malpractice insurance carrier to advise the carrier of what happened which could lead to a claim at a later date. I also believe that the attorney should notify the client notwithstanding any language to the contrary in the insurance policy. In the potential claim letter, the insured attorney should advise his or her malpractice insurance carrier of the fact that an application will be made to the court seeking to restore the client's matter to the active calendar list. Alternatively, if it's defense counsel whose answer has been stricken as a result of the insured's counsel's failure to answer interrogatories, the insured attorney should advise the malpractice carrier that an application will be made to restore the answer to its proper form by answering the interrogatories.

Unfortunately, in most cases, the legal malpractice insurance carrier ignores the letter of a potential claim. At best, a letter is sent to the insured attorney asking for a follow-up status within a specified period of time. This may be within six months. A diary note is placed on a file and later an examination, presumably by another adjustor, is made of the claim file to determine whether or not it should be closed or left open for future activity. In many instances, the claims hierarchy will insist upon closing these files. Often a claims examiner who is seeking to improve statistics will close a substantial number of these types of files.

By handling claims in this way, the legal malpractice insurance carrier jeopardizes its position with respect to insurance coverage. Despite case law throughout the United States which mandates that insurance carriers act with due diligence in asserting any rights they may have to non-coverage, the legal malpractice insurance carriers historically ignore that admonition. The traditional legal malpractice insurance market refuses to employ highly skilled experts to properly investigate claims when potential notices are received. In fact, as we will see later in this chapter, the legal malpractice insurance industry is ill-equipped to even investigate coverage issues from complaints that are filed on a first notice basis. For now, however, let us examine a 1982 New Jersey decision entitled, *Griggs v. Bertram* which may be found at 88 N.J. 347 (1982). The New Jersey Supreme Court, in a six-to-one decision, set forth a standard in New Jersey for the handling of potential claims of this nature.

In summary form, Bertram, on May 4, 1974, struck Griggs in a fight. After a short time, Bertram notified his insurance carrier. In August, an investigator for the insurance carrier interviewed Bertram, who admitted that he had punched Griggs twice. On December 4, a claim letter was sent by the insurance carrier, namely, Franklin Mutual. The carrier chose to do nothing from December 4, 1974 until a complaint was received in January 1976. On February 23, 1976 the carrier disclaimed coverage by advising Bertram it would not pay damages to Griggs, neither would it defend Bertram in a suit by Griggs. The New Jersey Supreme Court, in *Griggs*, held:

Upon the receipt from its insured of a claim or a notification of an incident that may give rise to a claim, an insurer is entitled to a reasonable period of time in which to investigate whether the particular incident involves a risk covered by the terms of the policy . . . But once an insurer has a reasonable opportunity to investigate, or has learned of grounds for questioning coverage, it then is under a duty promptly to inform its insured of its intention to disclaim coverage or of the possibility that coverage will be denied or questioned . . . Unreasonable delay in disclaiming coverage, or in giving notice of the possibility of such disclaimer, even before assuming actual control of a case or a defense of an action, can estop an insurer from later repudiating responsibility under the insurance policy. — *Griggs v. Bertram*, 88 NJ 347, at page 357.

The Court then held: "We therefore conclude that where, after timely notice, adequate opportunity to investigate a claim, and the knowledge of a basis for denying or questioning insurance coverage, the insurance carrier fails for an unreasonable time to inform the insured of a potential disclaimer, it is estopped from later denying coverage under the insurance policy in the event of a legal action is subsequently brought against its insured". — *id.*, pages 363-364.

While there are a number of factors involved in the *Griggs v. Bertram* case, the decision indicates that the seventeen-month delay by the insurance company caused the carrier to be equitably estopped from denying coverage. Many insurance personnel rely upon a statement that the courts cannot create coverage where none exists. The *Griggs v. Bertram* case is a noted exception to that principle. Insurers beware!

The other method of reporting claims arises out of an insured attorney's forwarding a summons and complaint which was filed in connection with a legal malpractice proceeding. Theoretically, the insured attorney is obligated to provide all of the information which is obtainable regarding the claim. This includes the summons and complaint, which are forwarded to the legal malpractice insurance carrier with a brief explanation attached. As a matter of time being of the essence, the insured attorney wishing to have an answer filed on his or her behalf will expedite the processing of these suit papers.

Many insurance carriers specify that all coverage issues must be reviewed by either a claims manager or by a coverage specialist. Too often, if this is done, it is without any precision. The examiner or adjustor who receives the first notice summons and complaint generally reviews the complaint and determines whether or not all of the allegations contained therein are within the ambit of coverage. Few independent investigations are made in order to determine any facts and circumstances beyond the scope of what is read or contained in or otherwise attached as exhibits to the summons and complaint. The adjustor or examiner at the first level barely has adequate time to review the complaint and process the paperwork necessary in connection with the handling of the claim. Ideally, the examiner or the adjustor would contact the insured attorney, review the entire file, assign an independent investigator where appropriate, and make all of the decisions concerning coverage right at this first level in the claims hierarchy process. In all of my years of experience, I have never encountered a legal malpractice insurance company that handles claims in this optimum fashion. Rather, what I usually see is a cursory review of the complaint.

A growing number of legal malpractice cases involve plaintiffs who sue both for covered and non-covered grounds. In other words, there are allegations against the insured attorney that fall both within and outside the scope of the insured's malpractice insurance coverage. To clarify this, let's first trace the steps in a case where the plaintiff is suing for covered grounds. Assume for a moment that a complaint alleges facts which fall squarely within the scope of coverage. Let's assume further that there are no allegations of an award or judgment in excess of the policy limits, nor are there any allegations of punitive damages which may be excluded under the policy. The allegations contained in the complaint are that the insured attorney was negligent in the performance of his or her duties. Furthermore, there is a claims made policy, the claim is made against the attorney during the policy period, and it is reported to the insurance carrier during the policy period. This situation is not difficult for an examiner handling legal malpractice cases. The examiner simply acknowledges receipt of the claim, sets forth the policy limits that are applicable, and assigns the case to defense counsel. We are assuming also that the case cannot be settled at this posture of the proceedings. The case would be assigned to either a house counsel operation or to an attorney who is on the approved list of panel attorneys handling the defense of these claims. The real dilemma, however, arises when there are both covered and non-covered grounds, as mentioned before. Let's now examine each option that is available to the claims department in response to this specific phenomenon.

THE RESERVATION OF RIGHTS

IN THE preceding section we examined how a complaint is handled when there are no coverage issues and when there is timely notice to the insurance carrier, under the terms and conditions of the lawyers' professional liability policy. The dilemma arises for the claims examiner when there are both covered and non-covered grounds alleged in a complaint. A basic example of what is referred to as "covered and non-covered grounds" should clarify this.

Mr. and Mrs. Injured-Party are passengers in a vehicle involved in a motor vehicle accident. Both Mr. and Mrs. Injured-Party suffered damages as a result of the automobile accident. They both see Mr. Malpractice Attorney who agrees to represent them. A number of years go by. Mr. and Mrs. Injured-Party from time to time call Mr. Malpractice Attorney to ask about the status of their case. Mr. Malpractice Attorney, however, continually ignores their calls. The secretaries working in Mr. Malpractice Attorney's office advise the clients that the matter is proceeding as scheduled. Let's assume Mr. Malpractice Attorney instructs his secretaries to so advise the clients. Further in our scenario of events, Mr. Malpractice Attorney allows the statute of limitations to expire. In other words, the time limit on filing the claim has expired. Thus, Mr. and Mrs. Injured-Party are permanently barred from making a claim against the parties responsible for the automobile accident.

At some point in time, Mr. Malpractice Attorney realizes that the statute of limitations has expired. Mr. Malpractice Attorney, like many other lawyers, decides to conceal his error from his clients. So when his clients telephone him to check on the status of the matter, he finally speaks with them, but advises that the case is on going and says that he will notify the clients when their case is finally reached for trial. There are many possible reasons for Mr. Malpractice Attorney's failure to disclose the fact that the statute of limitations has expired. We have observed in preceding chapters that many attorneys respond to a notice of claim by denying it exists. In our hypothetical set of circumstances, Mr. Malpractice Attorney probably believes that he will be able to resolve the matter on his own at some future date. He is also embarrassed to inform his malpractice carrier as well as his colleagues and clients of his error. Mr. Malpractice Attorney is also fearful that his legal malpractice insurance policy will be in jeopardy as a result of his conduct in this hypothetical case. Eventually, however, the victims of the legal malpractice, Mr. and Mrs. Injured-Party, will learn of the failure of Mr. Malpractice Attorney to file their action in a timely fashion. Mr. Malpractice Attorney was negligent. Now he has lied to the clients. Finally Mr. and Mrs. Injured-Party seek the advice of another attorney, who agrees to file suit against Mr. Malpractice Attorney for his conduct.

At this point in time, the new attorney must make a decision concerning what causes of action should be filed against Mr. Malpractice Attorney for his mishandling of the Mr. and Mrs. Injured-Party versus negligent automobile driver case. According to my definition of legal malpractice, there is no doubt that Mr. Malpractice Attorney has committed an omission in his failing to render professional services for others. There can be no doubt that Mr. Malpractice Attorney is also guilty under the standard traditional notions of negligence. He had a duty to file a claim within the applicable statute of limitations. He breached his duty to the clients by failing to do so. Now, the clients have suffered damages or harm as a result of Mr. Malpractice Attorney's negligence. Mr. and Mrs. Injured-Party are now unable to recover, from the negligent automobile driver, money for damages caused in the automobile accident.

At this point, the real question to address is whether or not the new attorney will file a lawsuit for both the negligence and the legal malpractice and the concealment, fraud, or misrepresentation which occurred prior to and subsequent to the expiration of the statute of limitations. In other words, Mr. Malpractice Attorney's concealing and misrepresenting the true status of the matter from his clients constitute separate and distinct causes of action which gives rise to damages. If the new attorney should file suit for fraud, misrepresentation, concealment, deceit, or any other related cause of action, the recovery from those causes of action may not be covered by the policy of insurance. The legal malpractice insurance policy may specifically exclude acts such as fraud, intentional conduct, and so on. The new attorney may also seek damages for emotional distress, punitive damages, and other damages which flow as a result of Mr. Malpractice Attorney's conduct. These additional damages may not be recoverable since the policy of insurance may very well exclude punitive damages or other types of damages. Therefore, we have acts on part of Mr. Malpractice Attorney which include covered grounds, namely, negligent acts, and we may have non-covered acts which include fraud, misrepresentation, and other allegations that fall outside the scope of the insurance coverage. It is in this context that we now examine the insurance carrier's response.

Typically, the examiner who first adjusts the claim reviews a complaint and summons filed against Mr. Malpractice Attorney. At this time, it should be apparent to the examiner that there are allegations that fall both within and outside the scope of insurance coverage. Usually, the examiner then issues what is commonly referred to as a "reservation of rights letter."

Many of these reservation of rights letters, which are sent to insured attorneys having insurance with the major legal malpractice insurance carriers, are invalid. As you will now see, these reservation of rights letters do not conform to what decisional law has mandated. In other words, courts throughout the United States have set standards for the issuance of these letters. Unfortunately, the insurance industry has failed or refused to follow those standards. It has consistently ignored decisional law in an effort to avoid its responsibilities concerning the issuance of letters of this type. Let's now examine a typical reservation of rights letter.

The examiner or adjustor who first handles the claim writes the insured a reservation of rights letter acknowledging receipt of the claim. Many times the adjustor will simply acknowledge receipt of the summons and complaint which was forwarded by the attorney for coverage under a specific insurance policy number. The adjustor will write to the lawyer detailing both the dollar limits of insurance and the applicable deductible. Next the examiner will recite in this letter the allegations contained in the complaint which was forwarded to the insurance company. The examiner may say there are allegations in the complaint that are clearly covered, let's say referable to negligence on the part of the lawyer. The examiner will then review those paragraphs of the complaint which contain allegations that are not covered by the policy of insurance. The examiner will say in this reservation of rights letter that one of the paragraphs in the complaint charges, let's say, fraud. This type of allegation, the examiner's letter should then go on to note, is specifically excluded from insurance coverage by the insurance policy. Generally, the relevant exclusion provisions of the policy are recited in the typical reservation of rights letter.

At this point controversy about the reservation of rights letter begins. Usually the examiner says that those portions of the complaint that seek damages for conduct which is not covered by the policy of insurance will be the sole and exclusive responsibility of the insured attorney. The typical reservation of rights letter says that the insured attorney may wish to retain counsel at his or her own expense to protect his or her own interest when facing these allegations. The reservation of rights letter also designates defense counsel assigned by the insurance company to presumably protect the interest of the insured attorney. As a practical matter, the reservation of rights letter also includes a section advising the insured to contact the examiner if he or she has any questions. This type of reservation of rights ultimately creates a strange alliance between the plaintiff's attorney, who is suing the lawyer insured by the insurance carrier, and the personal counsel who will represent the insured's interest in connection with a lawsuit of this type. Under these circumstances, the reservation of rights is generally deemed to be invalid. Thus, the insured attorney's personal counsel should then approach the plaintiff's counsel to discuss the respective interests each may have. They will try to persuade the insurance company that the carrier has responsibility to cover all of the damages arising out of the insured attorney's conduct in the handling of the underlying case.

This area of the law is highly technical. I have taken some case law from the New Jersey courts to illustrate what takes place when the insurance carrier issues its typical reservation of rights letters. These illustrations will further demonstrate this rather intricate aspect of the law and how it may apply to lawyers' professional liability claims.

The case of *Merchants Ind. Corp. v. Eggleston,* which may be found at 37 N.J. 114 (1962), introduced a standard that has been employed in issuing the reservation of rights letter. While the *Merchants* case did not involve a lawyers' professional liability claim, it did set the standard by which the insurance industry must react when it seeks to issue a reservation of rights letter. In a summary form, the *Merchants* case involved an insurance carrier by the same name, which was seeking a declaratory action to avoid its obligation to defend and indemnify an insured arising out of what was claimed to be a material misrepresentation of an ownership of an automobile insurance policy. The Supreme Court of New Jersey recited the facts and determined that within two weeks after the accident, the insurance company received a statement from its insured regarding the events of the accident. The statement was taken in May 1958. In October 1958, a damage action was filed against the insured in connection with the underlying automobile accident. An attorney assigned by the insurance company filed an answer on behalf of the insured to the underlying case in November 1958. In January 1959 the insurance company first officially disputed insurance coverage concerning the accident. In other words, the insurance company did not want to pay for the defense of the insured or for any loss on behalf of its insured. The insurance company then filed a declaratory action. In its lawsuit (which is referred to as the "declaratory action") the insurance company sought to avoid paying the defense and indemnity obligations arising out of the issuance of the insurance policy. A summons was issued and later served in February 1959 for this declaratory relief, seeking an adjudication of the insurance policy. The insurance company sued its insured, asking the court to issue a ruling that the insurance company was not responsible.

The Supreme Court noted that nine months passed between the time that the insurance company learned of the accident in underlying case and the time it first denied liability under the policy. In the interim, the insurance company continued with the defense of the lawsuit which arose in the underlying action. As is frequently the case, the insurance company did indeed continue with the defense of the case but it did so without issuing a reservation of rights letter. The Supreme Court of New Jersey held that the defense of the underlying case against the insured is incompatible with the denial of liability unless the insurance carrier reserves its rights (*id.,*page 126). The Supreme Court went on to say that the classic method of doing this is a non-waiver agreement. If the insurance company issues a proper reservation of rights letter and if the insured attorney fails to reject the insurance company's offer to defend the case under a reservation of rights, a non-waiver agreement may be inferred (*id.*). If the insurance carrier wishes to issue a reservation of rights letter and infer from the insured's failure to reject the offer of the reservation of rights, it must issue a reservation of rights letter which informs the insured that the offer may be accepted or rejected. In the *Merchants* case, the Court went on to say that if an insurance carrier fails to properly reserve its rights at the outset of a case, it will be deemed to have waived its right to claim misrepresentation or fraud in the inception of an insurance policy. So, if an insured attorney misrepresents or commits fraud in the application process, the insurance carrier will have waived its rights to seek a revision of that policy or any other remedy which may be available unless it properly reserves its rights under the terms and conditions of the insurance policy. Clearly, taking on the defense of the case without properly reserving its rights will constitute a waiver by the insurance carrier of its rights to seek any other remedy in connection with the proceedings.

In another New Jersey case entitled *Burd v. Sussex Mutual Insurance Company,* 56 NJ 383 (1970), the Supreme Court addressed the issue of the insurance carrier's obligation when there are allegations in a complaint which may not be covered under the insurance policy. Once again, we do not have a lawyers' professional liability lawsuit in this case, but the principles apply with equal persuasion to lawyers' professional liability lawsuits. In *Burd,* the Supreme Court of New Jersey reiterated its position that the control of defense is incompatible with a denial of liability unless the carrier has specifically reserved its rights to do so. This reservation would have to be agreed upon by the insured. The Court also stated that the duty to defend the insured may depend upon facts which are not set forth by the allegations in the complaint. It held that an insurance carrier may not prejudice the insured by defending the insured and controlling the defense of the case, and then later denying coverage, unless the insured has specifically agreed to such an arrangement. In the absence of such an agreement, the insurance carrier may be estopped from disputing coverage if it controls the defense of the case. The Supreme Court suggested that when the carrier's position is in conflict with the insured's position, and the insurance carrier cannot defend the action with what is characterized as "complete fidelity to the insured," there must be a proceeding in which the insured and the carrier literally fight out their differences, (*id.,* page 391). The Court said that, as in the *Burd* case, the insurance carrier may file a declaratory judgment action. This would follow the trial of the suit against the insured and it would determine the obligation of the insurance carrier. The Court also said that the insurance carrier's refusal to defend the suit because it sees an opportunity to avoid coverage will not deprive the insurance company to take a position, later, inconsistent with the insured with respect to insurance coverage.

My own view is that this policy making decision is a dangerous one for the insurance industry. If insurance companies are allowed to make the decision not to provide a defense to an insured, there will be abuses which will jeopardize the rights of insureds. Other jurisdictions have recognized such abuses, and allowed for the filing of bad faith litigation against insurance carriers for their refusal to defend and/or indemnify the insured under the terms of the insurance policy. An insurance carrier's wrongful refusal to defend and/or indemnify the insured's conduct will give rise (in many jurisdictions) to extra-contractual damages for such conduct by the carrier.

The only solution to this dilemma lies in the insurance industry's use of a non-waiver agreement when both covered and non-covered grounds are alleged against an insured attorney in a legal malpractice action. This non-waiver agreement should be handled by an expert in coverage who is either independently engaged by the insurance industry or, better yet, an employee of the insurance company who specializes in the negotiations of non-waiver agreements. The insurance carrier would simply dispatch the individual whenever allegations both covered and non-covered in nature are made against an insured in a complaint for damages. This highly skilled individual would negotiate with the insured so that both the insured and the insurance carrier could reserve rights under the terms and conditions of the policy. At the same time, the case could proceed without prejudicing the rights of the insured. This would then permit the insured attorney to reserve his or her rights to later seek the intervention of personal counsel on behalf of the insured attorney. Then the insurance carrier would also have the right, through the reservation agreement, to later disclaim coverage if subsequent investigation demonstrated that there were grounds for which the plaintiff or the claimant in the underlying case is seeking damages not covered by the policy of insurance. This process would also resolve the added dilemma of selection of defense counsel for the handling of the defense of the claim. This problem will again be addressed in the next chapter. During the course of the negotiations of a non-waiver agreement, the insured would, as a consequence of this agreement, agree that the insurance company would not be estopped later from raising any of its claims in connection with coverage issues. The insurance carrier would also, at the same time, reserve its rights and be deemed not have have waived any claim which it may argue gave rise to claims of fraud or misrepresentation in the inception of the insurance policy. In other words, if the insurance carrier believes that the insured attorney committed fraud in the inception of the insurance coverage through the application process, it could then take that position in this non-waiver agreement and attempt to seek a revision of the insurance policy for these misrepresentations. This type of reservation process would facilitate the working relationship between the insured attorney and the insurance carrier for the benefit of providing compensation to a victim of legal malpractice. Regrettably, these devices are rarely used. When I was employed by the insurance industry (and later served as consultant and counsel to the insurance industry), I frequently invoked this non-waiver agreement in handling major accounts insured under professional liability policies.

In my opinion, the use of these agreements neutralizes the climate that now exists of an adversarial relationship between the insured attorney and the insurance carrier.

In other words, by using the non-waiver agreement both the insured and the insurance carrier could work together to attempt to address the real issue: How much is the victim entitled to for damages? The alternative is the widespread litigation that we see today involving both the insured attorney and the insurance carrier. This type of chaotic, unstable atmosphere has resulted in bad faith causes of actions which are frequently leveled against the insurance carriers for their conduct, and which ultimately result in the victims having to wait even longer to recover their losses.

In the absence of a reservation or non-waiver agreement of this type, the control of the defense of these cases is quite chaotic. Consider, for a moment, what takes place when the selection of counsel is at issue and unresolved by both the insured attorney and the insurance carrier. Further information on this dilemma can be found in an article written in *For the Defense* by Walter Williamson entitled "Intervention by Insurers to Avoid Liability for Non-Covered Claims" (February 1983). The author describes the situation when both covered and non-covered grounds are alleged as a "vexing problem," one in which, as the author states, "it may be impossible to determine the extent to which sums were awarded for non-covered types of damages as opposed to covered types" (p. 19). Williamson suggests intervention by the insurance carrier as a means of solving this problem. As we will see, this idea has not received widespread acceptance. The reason appears to be the chaos that surrounds controlling the defense of a lawsuit. Even lawyers I lecture have difficulty understanding this technical aspect of the law. We will now see how this dilemma is resolved through the selection of defense counsel to defend lawyers charged with legal malpractice. ≡

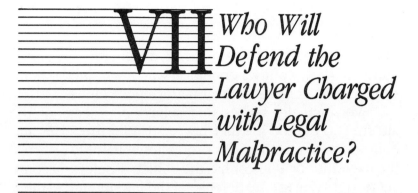

VII Who Will Defend the Lawyer Charged with Legal Malpractice?

AS THE litigation involving legal professional liability increases, so has the use of house or staff counsel to defend legal malpractice lawsuits. In theory, the house counsel operation consists of attorneys hired by the insurance company to set up a law firm separate and apart from the insurance company itself. In reality, this is merely legal fiction; usually the house counsel staff is supported entirely by the insurance company with whom it is associated. The basic reason behind this theoretical separation is to provide an unbiased entity for the assigning of defense for lawsuits arising out of legal professional liability matters. To economize in the defense of these lawsuits, insurance carriers have expanded the use of the house counsel operations and have been assigning to house counsel the defense of these claims on a more regular basis. In reality, most house counsel operations are ill-equipped to deal with this crisis of legal malpractice. When an examiner selects a house counsel operation (presuming it is the examiner who makes the selection), he usually has a difficult time finding a defense counsel who has a great deal of experience in handling legal malpractice claims. In most instances, the house counsel attorney is employed to handle a variety of matters including property and casualty lawsuits, product liability, and other areas of insurance matters. Rarely, if ever, do you find specialists within a house counsel operation who are trained specifically for the defense of legal malpractice claims.

Who actually makes this selection process of the attorney to defend another lawyer? Under the terms and conditions of most lawyers professional liability policies, the examiner or adjustor has the choice of selecting counsel responsible for the defense of the lawsuit unless there is a conflict of interest. There has been a flurry of conflict of interest litigation involving the propriety of using a house counsel operation, particularly in a lawyer's professional liability lawsuit. Unless there is a coverage dispute or, in the alternative, if a conflict, in fact, should arise, the use of house counsel is permitted. I advocate the use of a highly trained and skilled house and staff counsel operation as a means of reducing legal expenses within a legal malpractice program. Additionally, in many cases, a skilled defense lawyer will recognize the victim's right to compensation, thereby making it easier for the victim to recover. These skilled practitioners must be experts in legal malpractice lawsuits. Regrettably, the insurance companies, who have to compete with law firms, have, traditionally, been unwilling to pay the salaries necessary to attract the highest level of competent defense lawyers. As a consequence, the reputation of house counsel has been questioned, at least concerning the defense of legal malpractice claims. A possible solution would require the carrier to seek out a few top level individuals who have expertise in professional liability and pay them competitive salaries. In addition, the carrier should initiate a training program to allow second, third, and fourth level employees to handle the defense of routine legal malpractice matters. I am confident that such proper use of house counsel would help reduce the runaway costs of the defense of these claims, leaving more money to compensate the victims.

PANEL COUNSEL: TRIPARTITE OR TRIAD

MOST LAWSUITS filed against attorneys for legal malpractice or negligence are defended by what is commonly referred to as "panel counsel." These are law firms that have been selected by the insurance company to be on an approved list of attorneys to be assigned cases for defense by the claims department of the insurance company. In other words, when an examiner or adjustor receives a first notice complaint or summons which has been filed against an insured attorney, the claims examiner telephones one of the law firms which has been approved to defend these lawsuits. The examiner then assigns the defense of this particular case to that law firm. The process by which a law firm becomes an approved law firm designated as panel counsel for the defense of these cases varies from carrier to carrier. Generally, however, a law firm seeking to do professional liability defense work submits a resume to a claims manager for review. More important, the law firm seeking to attain entry to the defense panel's approved list must set forth rates which are substantially lower than commercial rates for litigation of this type. In the majority of instances, an insurance panel defense firm reduces its rates in order to receive a volume of assignments from one or more insurance carriers. In addition, many law firms seeking to obtain approval for defense of legal malpractice cases agree to defer billing for six months or a year or until the case closes. While some law firms handle a specialty line of legal malpractice cases, (e.g., Securities and Exchange or tax work), the majority of firms substantially compromise general billing practices and rates in exchange for receiving work of this type. From an economic standpoint, the carriers generally do not pay for defense bills on receipt. Instead, carriers usually take a long time to process the payment of bills or statements forwarded by the defense firms. The consequences of this prolonged process are obvious. From the outset, it becomes apparent that the defense panel will not have its higher echelon of partners or senior associates handling most of the legal malpractice defense cases. In many instances, lower level associates handle the nuts and bolts of the defense of these cases in order to make them economically feasible. I am critical of the present method of selecting a defense counsel panel, since it discourages the higher level partners from participating in this entire process. Instead, the insurance industry is basically underwriting the educational process for entry level associates of law firms. Indeed, if the matter is so basic as to allow for an entry level associate to devote a substantial amount of his or her time on the file, the case probably should have been disposed of by house or staff counsel in the first place.

The real question that an attorney, insured under a lawyers' professional liability policy, should ask himself or herself at the threshold of this inquiry is whether or not he or she wants a panel counsel attorney to defend the lawsuit. Under most circumstances, without a coverage issue or a conflict, the insured attorney has no choice. Once a coverage issue is raised or if there is another kind of conflict of interest, the insured attorney must then examine the tripartite or triad relationship which exists between the panel counsel, insurance carrier, and insured attorney.

For example, an insured attorney is sued for negligence, as well as for failure to file a claim within the applicable statute of limitations and fraud arising out of conduct both prior to the expiration of the statute of limitations and conduct subsequent to the expiration of the statute of limitations. Does that insured attorney want panel counsel defending him in those circumstances? The insured attorney might want to weigh or compare the panel counsel's expertise in handling only claims of this type against the economic realities that confront panel counsel. In my experience, all panel counsel represent insurance companies on coverage issues as well. Therefore, you truly do not have panel counsel who are completely independent in the defense of a lawsuit. While there is no question that the insured attorney is entitled to paramount loyalty from the panel counsel, in reality it does not always happen. One must consider the fact that panel counsel relies heavily upon the insurance company for economic survival. The majority of courts would recognize this dilemma and suggest that under such circumstances there is indeed a conflict and that an alternative resolution must be made in order to adequately protect the interest of the insured attorney. I have witnessed cases in which insurance carriers penalize a panel attorney who truly protects the interest of the insured. The underlying problems are deciding who can provide the best defense in these chaotic claims situations and how this defense process can function realistically. If the attorney committed a wrong against the client, which defense firm is more likely to be interested in an expedited resolution? In other words, who will want to pay the victim to have this case settled quickly without the need for a protracted litigation?

PERSONAL OR INDEPENDENT COUNSEL

THERE ARE some jurisdictions that have long recognized the right of an insured to select counsel of his or her own choice at the carrier's expense when there is in fact a conflict between the interests of the carrier and the interests of the insured. There has been so much discussion concerning this selection process and its implications that legislation has recently been enacted in California to set standards for this entire process. Most jurisdictions, however, do not deal with this issue on a legislative basis. Instead, this issue has been determined through the development of case law. For example, in New

Jersey, when there are both covered and non-covered grounds alleged in the complaint, and there exists a conflict of interest, it is established that the personal counsel may be the choice of the individual insured over the panel counsel selected by the insurance carrier. A case that has been referred to earlier in this book, *Merchants Indemnity Corp. v. Eggleston,* 37 NJ 114 (1962), recognizes this fact. The case states that:

> A carrier may be more confident of his handling of claims, but an insured may with equal conviction prefer the individualized attention of his own counsel as against the services furnished by an insurer in the mass handling of litigation. Personal counsel may seize opportunities to settle which might be ignored or overlooked by a carrier to which the case is just one of a great number. Moreover, whatever his estimate of lawyers in general, a man usually has faith in "my lawyer." This intangible is a valuable right" — 37 NJ 114; at page 127.

This statement brings up questions concerning the mechanisms and functioning of the independent counsel selection process. For example, Who pays? Another New Jersey Court decision has stated that in the event of a conflict, the insured should select counsel of its own choice and this choice must be approved by the insurance carrier (*Dunn v. Firemen's Fund Am. Ins. Company,* 69 NJ 244, 252 [1976]). In the event that the insurance carrier does not approve of the insured's selection of counsel, then an application must be made to the chief assignment judge of the territory . The selection is then made or confirmed by the assignment judge and the related legal fees and costs become the obligation of the insurance company. The courts in New Jersey have also indicated that special interrogatories should be submitted to determine the basis for liability, if any. Thus, in the example in which the insured attorney is sued for both fraud and negligence, presumably counsel would submit special interrogatories to a jury to determine which portion of the jury verdict was rendered on the fraud count and which portion was rendered on the negligence count. I question the effectiveness of this procedure since counsel selected by the insured or for that matter, independent counsel, would be obligated to bring in a verdict of straight negligence in order to insure that there is complete coverage for the loss for the benefit of the insured attorney. If counsel were to take any other position, it is my judgment he or she would be subject to a malpractice action. Therefore as a practical matter, many of these issues are still in their embryonic stages. While some jurisdictions, such as California, have litigated these cases on a regular basis, the courts in most other states are now, as a matter of first impression, beginning to face many of the issues underlying legal malpractice. Thus, we can expect that in most jurisdictions these issues will develop and undoubtedly litigation will result.

I have described this entire area of the law as being chaotic. In my own experience, I can recall one matter where I was brought into the case to represent an individual insured. He was being sued and a jury had awarded damages against this individual well beyond his policy limits. During the course of my representation of the insured, I opted to have panel counsel handle the appeal on behalf of my client. My reasons were simple: in this instance, panel counsel had excellent credentials in the insurance industry. Moreover, the insurance carrier controlled the defense of the case. To evidence this, when I was brought into the matter, I immediately discussed the prospects of settlement directly with the plaintiff's counsel. I had suggested that we perfect an assignment of interests in order to protect my client from the verdict which was rendered in excess of his insurance policy limits. The insurance carrier's representative, who was the claims manager at the time, heard this conversation and actually suggested that my client may be in breach of the cooperation clause of the insurance policy by discussing the prospects of settlement with the plaintiff's counsel. I decided that the insurance carrier's refusal to post bond for the excess award and its threat regarding my efforts at settling the claim were clear evidence of bad faith on the part of the insurance company. In any event, the case continued through the appellate process. At the appellate level hearing, there was a dispute over which attorney should represent the insured individual. Plaintiff's counsel, under the terms and conditions of an assignment, sought to have the appeal dismissed. In the confusion, the appellate panel actually recessed the hearing and called upon me to make a decision whether or not I wanted to take a substitution of attorney on behalf of my client and dismiss the action. In jurisdictions such as New Jersey where there are no set procedures, one can easily see how chaos becomes inevitable. The case ultimately settled.

My resolution of this dilemma starts with the carrier's employment of a highly skilled, trained investigator to determine coverage issues right from the outset of the proceedings. In the overwhelming majority of instances, the insurance carrier ultimately pays any resulting judgment. Therefore, I would implement a system in which the carrier would waive most of these issues concerning coverage, particularly when there are both covered and non-covered grounds alleged in the complaint. I would further recommend that the carrier agree to defend these cases and agree to indemnify against any resulting adverse judgment settlement or award. This would eliminate the use of the excessive number of attorneys in connection with these proceedings. Furthermore, it would also reduce any prospect of the carrier having to pay for coverage counsel as well as counsel for the insured in the event that the declaratory action is not successful.

All of this would leave more funds available to the victim.

Unfortunately, to date, no carrier has had the courage to modify its existing method of handling claims in order to approach the dilemma from a different, less chaotic perspective. I have consistently predicted that runaway legal expenses will be responsible for the failure on the part of many insurance companies to level off the rates of insurance in legal malpractice or negligence programs. These rates deprive the victim of the security of knowing there is sufficient insurance money available to pay for the mistakes of the negligent lawyer. ≡

VIII Defenses to a Legal Malpractice Claim

STATUTE OF LIMITATIONS

OF ALL the defenses available to a suit of legal malpractice, the statute of limitations is the most fundamental. It limits the amount of time within which a lawsuit must be brought for damages. The statute of limitations has its origins in an equitable principle which is referred to as "Laches:" if one has a right to sue an attorney in theory and fails or refuses to act on that right until the applicable statute of limitations has expired, one may be forever barred from pursuing any remedy which may be available. In legal malpractice, the statute of limitations varies in each jurisdiction. In other words, one must look to the particular state to determine which statute of limitations is applicable to legal malpractice actions in that state. Ordinarily, the state legislatures will enact laws which govern the statute of limitations with respect to different courses of conduct. Since legal malpractice is a recent phenomenon, the case law surrounding the statute of limitations has depended to a large extent on how the conduct underlying the malpractice has been classified by the courts in each state. For example, in some jurisdictions, legal malpractice is considered a contract right. In other jurisdictions, it is equated with a property right. Others still have looked upon legal malpractice as a personal injury right. In many jurisdictions, the courts have developed a discovery rule applicable to legal malpractice actions. The discovery rule is applied to extend the statute of limitations when a victim is not aware that he or she has a cause of action against a lawyer for legal malpractice. In some cases, the victim does not know of damage or injury or, in the alternative, does not know that there is a cause of action that exists or could not know that a cause of action existed against a lawyer.

A recent Appellate Division decision in New Jersey, *Mant v. Gillespie*, 189 NJ Super. 368 (App. Div. 1983) allowed for a discovery rule to extend the ordinary statute of limitations. The Court addressed when, in a legal malpractice action, clients ought to be aware that there was malpractice by an attorney. The Appellate Division analyzed the facts and circumstances with particular reference to when the cause of action begins to accrue. That is, When does the statute of limitations begin to run? Is it when the malpractice actually occurs or is it when damage is actually sustained? Let's examine the *Gillespie* decision to gain a better perspective of the issues raised in applying the applicable statute of limitations. The Appellate Court, at the outset of its decision, noted that in 1983 the applicable case law in New Jersey did not address the issue of when (for statute of limitation purposes) a legal malpractice action begins to accrue. The facts as noted in the complaint were that the plaintiffs, Mant, contracted with Healey for the purchase of certain property. The defendant in the legal malpractice action, namely, Gillespie, represented both parties in that transaction. After litigation between Healey and Mant, it was finally determined by the Appellate Division that the purchase money mortgage in which Gillespie represented both parties was invalid in that Healey did not have independent counsel. Healey was awarded damages in the amount of $30,000. Mant thereupon sought damages against Gillespie for the judgment of $30,000 plus counsel fees.

The Mants filed suit in February 1981. Gillespie

claimed a statute of limitations defense in that it was not instituted within six-year after the date of the malpractice. Both parties admitted that the six years statute of limitations applied in New Jersey for legal malpractice and further that the discovery rule was applicable as well. Once again, the discovery rule provides that a cause of action will not begin to accrue until a party discovers that there are indeed injuries (or damage) or should have discovered that there are injuries or damages which are actionable against the lawyer. The Court held that damage must indeed be sustained before the cause of action accrues.

As a rule applied to the facts of *Mant v. Gillespie,* the Appellate Division said that the trial court should have determined when the plaintiffs either actually were aware of the facts of the damage or ought to have been aware of the facts relating to damage caused by Gillespie. The Court went on to analyze the damage claim and separated it into two categories: the award of $30,000 against the Mants and the funds necessary to defend themselves in that lawsuit as being a separate damage. The Court held the award of $30,000 did not occur until November 1978, at which time the Court announced a judgment in favor of Healey. Therefore, applying the discovery rule, the Court held the following:

> Any accrual of the malpractice cause of action before November 27, 1978 can only be based, then, on a finding that the Mants knew or ought to have known that their legal expenses in defending the Healey transaction were or might be attributable to negligence of Gillespie — *id.,* page 374.

After an analysis of the facts and circumstances, the Appellate Division reversed the trial court and remanded the case for further proceedings in accordance with a discovery hearing. On remand, the trial court was directed to conduct this preliminary hearing on the statute of limitations issue, but it was left to the discretion of the trial court as to whether to proceed to trial and determine this issue at the end of all the proceedings, or make a preliminary determination.

Mant therefore stands for the proposition that there must be damage prior to an accrual of the cause of action from wrongful conduct.

Mallen, in his treatise on legal malpractice, opines that there are indeed two operative dates for statute of limitations which are: the wrongful act or omission and the actual injury (*Legal Malpractice*, 2nd Edition, 1981, p. 445.) Mallen however, does go on to say the statute of limitations may be tolled by certain statutes in each state. Each jurisdiction may have a statute which allows for the cause of action against the lawyer to begin to run when, let's say, a minor reaches the age of majority. In addition to those statutory provisions, there is, of course, the already referred to discovery rule, or the discovery of the concealment by the attorney, or the termination of the lawyer's representation — (*id.,* page 445).

There are practical problems in determining when the statute of limitations may begin to run against a lawyer for legal malpractice. Let's assume that some courts are correct in saying that you need damage to an injured party before a statute of limitations may begin to run. Let's take, for an example, a lawyer drafting a will on behalf of a client. The client dies some thirty years later. We now know that under the terms and conditions of a claims made lawyers' insurance policy, the lawyer would not have insurance coverage until such time as a claim is made against the lawyer and the lawyer in turn reports the claim to the insurance company. In our will situation, there may be a lapse of twenty or thirty years before a claim is made against the attorney. Of course, a preliminary question may be, Where is the attorney now? Attention may then be turned to, Is the attorney still practicing law? The real question, however, is Does the statute of limitations first begin to run some twenty or thirty years after the will was drafted? It would seem that in order to avoid inequitable results, there have to be creative solutions to these problems.

There are a number of other issues that need to be addressed in connection with the statute of limitations. If, during the course of handling a matter a lawyer commits several errors or omissions, the question then becomes, Does the statute of limitations begin to run when the first act of malpractice occurs or the last act of malpractice? These issues are easily confused with the argument that the claim of legal malpractice does not mature into a legitimate cause of action against the lawyer until there is damage or injury.

Legal malpractice cases are litigated frequently as a consequence of divided opinions regarding these issues. When the lawyer who is negligent presents the defense of the statute of limitations, be prepared for extended litigation — particularly in those cases where there is a discovery rule where the victim is chargeable with actual knowledge or constructive knowledge of when legal malpractice occurred. Undoubtedly, there will be litigation over those issues. We will certainly see the development of these issues and a more definitive statement of the law as these cases reach the highest court in each jurisdiction.

CONTRIBUTORY & COMPARATIVE NEGLIGENCE

WHEN WE speak of contributory or comparative negligence, we are dealing with a defense to a legal malpractice law suit. It is the degree of fault on the part of client-victim which may defeat or otherwise reduce the client-victim's recovery of damages, which the client-victim would otherwise have been entitled to receive. Depending upon the state in which a law suit is litigated, it may be that contributory negligence, if it is held applicable to a legal malpractice action, may bar a client from recovering against a former attorney. In other jurisdictions, comparative negligence, if found applicable, may only reduce the amount of recovery by the comparative degree of the client's responsibility. Let's use an example. Let's say that a client who is involved in a car accident case visits an attorney's office and the attorney is prepared to undertake the representation of the client. The client thereafter refuses to provide necessary information to the attorney. The attorney, therefore, is not able to file suit on the client's behalf. The attorney makes repeated requests to the client, but the client steadfastly refuses to provide the information. After the expiration of the statute of limitations, the client sues the attorney for the attorney's failure to file the case within the applicable time period. The attorney would set up as a defense the fact that the client was contributorily negligent. In some jurisdictions that would defeat the client's cause. In other jurisdictions, the degree of fault on part of the client would be compared to the degree of fault on part of the lawyer, and the result would be dependent upon the jury's findings of a percentage of fault. The amount of recovery or award would then be molded by the percentage of fault by each respective party. If, for example, in some jurisdictions where comparative negligence is applied, the jury finds the plaintiff's degree of fault or negligence less than the lawyer's degree of fault or negligence, the plaintiff may recover. Specifically, let's assume the jury awards $100,000 for damages to a plaintiff but finds the plaintiff to be 40 percent at fault and the lawyer to be 60 percent at fault. The judge would then mold the verdict to allow for the plaintiff to recover only $60,000 of the $100,000 damage award. The degree of fault on part of the plaintiff would reduce by 40 percent the amount that the jury awarded for damages. In other jurisdictions, where a strict contributory negligence theory is applied, the plaintiff's case against the lawyer may be lost if the jury finds the plaintiff was negligent to any extent or if the jury finds that the plaintiff's conduct was a substantial factor in bringing about the result. One could argue that these defenses of contributory and comparative negligence should not be available when a lawyer is sued for legal malpractice, as a matter of public policy. In other words, there should be no basis for allowing a lawyer to either avoid responsibility or to reduce the amount of the verdict by the conduct of the plaintiff. I believe a persuasive argument may be made to abolish these defenses as they apply to legal malpractice actions.

NO ATTORNEY-CLIENT RELATIONSHIP

IN PRACTICE, the defense used most often by lawyers is what they claim to be "no attorney-client relationship" between the lawyer and the client. Generally, this will take two forms. The first will be the fact that the attorney and the client are not in a relationship of privity. The attorney would seek to defend his or her conduct on the basis that there is no contract running between the attorney and the client. This defense is no longer favored by most courts. There are, however, some courts in some states that will allow this type of defense to be used in connection with a legal malpractice lawsuit.

Let's again look at a typical example. Mr. and Mrs. Client seek to purchase a home which is a two-family residence. They go directly to the township attorney who is employed by the township to seek an opinion as to whether or not the two-story dwelling is a permitted use of the premises according to the township zoning ordinances. The township attorney issues an opinion that indeed the house is within the accepted boundaries of the zoning ordinance. The couple then proceeds to purchase the home and move in. At some later date another township official files a complaint against the couple seeking to have the two-family home declared an unlawful use. The township official decides that there should only be single-family dwellings in the neighborhood. The couple then attempts to sue the township attorney, who now takes the position that there was no privity with Mr. and Mrs. Client; that is, that as township attorney he had no direct client-attorney relationship.

Most courts are now moving to the proposition that if the attorney gives the advice and it is foreseeable that victims such as Mr. and Mrs. Client may rely upon that advice, there is a cause of action for legal malpractice against the township attorney. In our example, Mr. and Mrs. Client undoubtedly did rely upon the advice of the township attorney. Moreover, the township attorney at the time of giving the couple the advice knew, or should have known, and it would be foreseeable, that the couple would rely upon that advice to their detriment.

Another example of this would be Mr. and Mrs. Client purchasing a home through a lending institution which provides a mortgage. The lending institution has an attorney who purports to review all the documents relating to the purchase and insures that everything is in proper order prior to the closing of title. Mr. and Mrs. Client do not have independent legal advice. After they purchase their home, they learn that there is an easement running through their property which no one brought to their attention prior to the closing of title. The couple now wants to sue the attorney who represented the bank and appeared at the closing. Their theory of recovery is based on the fact that they paid the attorney for his review of the documents, and therefore they established an attorney-client relationship. The attorney denies the attorney-client relationship and claims he is merely the attorney for the bank and at no time was he employed by the couple in connection with the review of the documents. The courts are divided on this issue as well. If we use our standard test as to whether or not reliance on the advice given was foreseeable, and that the couple did rely upon it and did indeed rely upon it to their detriment, it would seem to satisfy all these requirements. The courts, however, remain divided on this issue.

A second aspect of the form of attorney-client relationship involves an attorney who refuses to acknowledge that there is an attorney-client relationship. I have been called in on many cases in which this has happened. For example, in one case an elderly woman went to see an attorney after suffering from an accident. The client gave the attorney the information, expecting to have the attorney handle the investigation and make the prompt and efficient settlement of the claim, or in the alternative, place the matter into suit if a settlement was not reached. The client called the attorney on a number of occasions to check on the status of the matter. It was only several years after the accident that the client realized the attorney never filed a lawsuit on her behalf. Her repeated phone calls were met by a receptionist's response that the matter was well in hand. At no time was the client informed that the attorney was not undertaking the matter as her counsel. The statute of limitations expired. The client was forever barred from filing suit. When the client sued the attorney, the attorney claimed that he was never retained. There was no formal retainer agreement entered into. The attorney argued that the client was barred from recovery. This defense is one that is often utilized by attorneys after they are sued by a former client for failing to file claims within the applicable statute of limitations.

JUDGMENTAL RULE

THE GREATEST myth in lawyer's defense of legal malpractice lawsuits involves a judgment call in making a decision concerning a client's case. We see this often after a settlement of a case in which the client later seeks to sue the attorney for improper advice. The client is dissatisfied with the settlement. The attorney will frequently defend him or herself on the theory that the client may not sue the attorney for an error in judgment. I frequently respond to that defense by saying it is how the judgment call is made that determines whether or not there is legal malpractice. I am frequently called upon by clients to evaluate whether or not a judgment was proper by an attorney in a particular case. I generally look first at the method used by the attorney to arrive at a particular judgment. If indeed the attorney did not do his or her homework in connection with gathering the investigative reports and did not undertake the proper legal research, there is no doubt in my mind that judgment was arrived at through negligence on the part of the attorney. That negligence would be the basis of a legal malpractice lawsuit.

Let's say, for example, the attorney, in determining whether or not to settle a personal injury case, believes that the law allows for the defense of comparative negligence. The lawyer evaluates the client's chances at recover at roughly 50 percent. He therefore places a value of 50 percent of the recovery on the client's claim. If the lawyer is mistaken about the law governing comparative negligence, his obvious conclusion would be mistaken as well. Therefore, one has to examine what takes place at the very first part of the case and trace all of the steps which an attorney took in determining whether or not the judgment call was a proper one. Contrary to popular belief amongst lawyers, an error in judgment may result in legal malpractice.

OTHER DEFENSES

ONE OF the most frequently used defenses by lawyers involves the use of a release. At the outset, I believe that it is highly inappropriate for a lawyer to use a release with a client. While a release does not automatically violate the direct rules of ethics, its use in the future may, in fact, constitute such a violation. An attorney will, as a practical matter, seek a release from the client, or mutual releases from various clients, in connection with the settlement of claims. The attorneys will insist that the clients execute mutual releases in order to relieve the lawyers of future liability. This entire process is suspect.

Attorneys may also seek to employ other means to guard against liability to clients. Many of the defenses I see rely upon complex legal theories such as indemnification, contribution, fault of other counsel, disclaimer, ratification, immunity, privilege, res judicata, collateral estoppel, compromise with third party. While it may not be necessary to identify the specific circumstance where each one of these defenses may apply, it is important to understand that these defenses may be available to attorneys and are frequently used in connection with legal malpractice proceedings. ≡

IX Trial of a Legal Malpractice Case

TRIAL & USE OF EXPERTS

THE TRIAL of a legal malpractice case has been referred to as "a land of second changes." (Mallen and Levit, *Legal Malpractice*, 2nd edition, West Publishing Co., 1981, p. 791) This is an appropriate description. Since the handling of legal malpractice cases is such a rapidly growing aspect of the law, authorities often differ regarding how a legal malpractice case should be tried. In addition, the rules governing the standards of recovery vary from state to state. The traditional approach to a legal malpractice trial can be considered a "trial within a trial" or "case within a case." This means there are two primary objectives for the jury in a legal malpractice case: the first is to determine whether or not there was negligence on the part of the attorney in the handling of the underlying case; and second, the jury must determine either what the outcome should have been or would have been in the underlying case in order to establish what damages the plaintiff would be entitled to. This has also been referred to as a "but for" test; that is to say, how much would the victim of a legal malpractice have recovered but for the attorney's negligence, or would the defendant have prevailed in the underlying case but for the attorney's negligence. I have often criticized the traditional approach to legal malpractice and the use of these rigid standards since there is no consideration for the value of the client's loss of opportunity or for the value of any foregone success. This should be one of the jury's concerns, but it is not when one applies these standards. By the use of these tests, the trial of the legal malpractice action is unnecessarily complicated.

In a trial a juror must be a fact finder. This means each juror must determine the facts in the case and the entire jury must base its decision on those facts. The judge's role is to apply the law. The judge also instructs the jury on the law and directs the jury to make specific findings of fact consistent with the law. Thus, in a legal malpractice trial, the crux of the entire action is what evidence will be admitted during the trial. This evidence will ultimately decide whether or not the attorney is guilty of malpractice. Generally, as I have already indicated in Chapter III, the term "legal malpractice" will be defined by the courts as the failure of an attorney to use and exercise such skill, prudence, and diligence as other members of the legal profession commonly possess and exercise in representing clients. In the context of an actual case, the plaintiff will have to establish, by what is referred to as "a preponderance of the evidence," a duty on part of the defendant attorney. Then the plaintiff must show a breach of that duty and a proximate cause relationship between the breach of the duty and the actual damage which the plaintiff suffered as a result of that breach. These are the standards by which a party must prove a legal malpractice case. Legal malpractice should be determined according to whether or not the plaintiff has established, by a preponderance of the evidence, that the attorney committed an act, error, or omission in rendering or failing to render professional services which results in damages or harm to the client. Regardless of how legal malpractice is defined, a plaintiff must nevertheless establish that there are certain standards by which attorneys conduct themselves. The plaintiff must then go on to show a deviation from those standards. The real question is, How is this accomplished? The answer, in most cases, is by the use of expert testimony.

Generally, experts testify during the course of legal malpractice trials. In my experience, I have called upon two experts on behalf of the plaintiffs I represent. Generally, the first expert is someone who is recognized as an authority on professional responsibility or legal ethics. The second expert usually deals with the substantive aspects of the law. This means that if a plaintiff is suing a lawyer for that lawyer's mishandling of a personal injury case, I produce one expert in professional responsibility or legal ethics and a second expert who is a leading authority in the area of personal injury litigation. The expert on professional responsibility or legal ethics testifies as to what the attorney's responsibility was in the handling of a particular matter. If there are ethical breaches involved, the expert also testifies specifically as to what these breaches were. This way the judge can direct the jury to find negligence as a result of those specific standards having been breached. The expert who is the authority in personal injury litigation is then called on to testify as to the standard of care which would be demanded or expected of an attorney in the handling of personal injury matters. The use of these experts has caused considerable controversy, especially with regard to the scope of permitted testimony. First, Should the experts be allowed to testify regarding the outcome of the original case had it been tried without any legal malpractice? For example, take an attorney who fails to file a claim within the applicable statute of limitations. Should an expert be allowed to testify as to what the jury would have decided in the underlying case? While the trial within a trial practice is established, most courts would not allow an expert to speculate or otherwise predict what the outcome would have been in the underlying case, "but for" the legal malpractice. Rather confusingly, the jury would have to be subject to a re-creation of the first trial. The jury would then have to place itself in the position of the fact finder in the original trial. In other words, the second jury in the legal malpractice case is placed in the position of the first jury in the underlying case, in order to determine what the first jury should, or would have, done had the case been handled correctly. A small minority of courts have allowed experts to testify as to what the jury would have done, mainly because there have been no objections by any party to the admission of that type of testimony.

The traditional trial within a trial approach in the context of legal malpractice raises additional expert testimony issues. For instance, are the experts to be permitted to testify as to what the case would have settled for had there been no legal malpractice? It is common knowledge that the overwhelming majority of cases are ultimately settled. Would an expert then be permitted to testify as to what the likely settlement value of a case would be had there been no legal malpractice? At the present time these issues have not been clearly decided. We do know, however, that the traditional trial within a trial approach has been criticized since it ignores the possibility of settlement. (See *Gautam v. DeLuca,* 215 NJ Super. 388, 398 [App. Div. 1987]).

To clarify this criticism, consider a New Jersey case which disapproves of the trial within a trial technique as being an absolute standard. The case of *Lieberman v. Employers Mutual Insurance Company of Wausau,* (84 NJ 325, 1980) involved a physician who was sued for medical malpractice. The insurance company which covered the physician, namely Lieberman, for medical malpractice assigned an attorney to defend Dr. Lieberman in the medical malpractice case. The attorney entered into a settlement over Dr. Lieberman's objections. Dr. Lieberman then sued the attorney for legal malpractice. The Supreme Court of New Jersey disapproved of the strict trial within a trial approach as a standard for every case. The Court said it would be "awkward and impractical" to now have Lieberman, who was a defendant in the medical malpractice case, to be placed as a plaintiff in the legal malpractice case under the traditional notions of a trial within a trial approach. The Supreme Court went on to say that this type of an approach would "skew" so that the legal malpractice trial would not really mirror or parallel the earlier trial (*id.*, page 43). The court also noted parenthetically that the passage of time may be a factor which would work against applying a trial within a trial approach. The Court went on to say it would be up to the trial judge (absent an agreement between parties) as to the method and manner in which the legal malpractice case would be tried. Experts would then be allowed to testify if they were able to determine, with reasonable probability, what would have transpired within the original trial (*id.*, page 344).

There are also legal malpractice cases in which expert testimony is not required. For instance, if the evidence is within the common experience and knowledge of the jurors, expert testimony may not be required. I do, however, recommend the use of experts in every legal malpractice case.

In addition, there may be a "bifurcation" of the legal malpractice trial. This means that the trial would be split into two distinct and separate proceedings. The first proceeding would concern the issue of whether or not there was negligence on the part of the attorney, and the second proceeding would determine the damages which may be applicable. These questions and variations regarding the issues and proceedings in a legal malpractice trial reflect and emphasize the uncertainty which surrounds this aspect of the law.

DAMAGES

THE GENERAL rule is that the attorney is liable for damages that are proximately caused by his negligence. Thus it follows the plaintiff has the burden of proof of those damages by what is referred to as a "preponderance of the evidence." In most jurisdictions the only damages recoverable are those which are a direct and proximate result of the attorney's negligence. In the majority of the jurisdictions, the only damages which are recoverable by the plaintiffs are those which are direct damages flowing from the attorney's negligence. Whether or not any additional damages, for instance, consequential damages, are the attorney's responsibility is an issue that is not clear or well settled in all jurisdictions. Consider, for example, an attorney who fails to file a claim for the collection of a debt which is known to be a fixed amount of money. The amount of damage would be the amount of money which the attorney was to collect, excluding any consideration for interest, costs, or such. The recovery is based on the assumption that the amount is collectible from a defendant-debtor. In addition, there are guidelines concerning other damages such as consequential damages or damages for the infliction of emotional distress. Generally, you must show a special grievance or special harm in order to establish additional damages in legal malpractice actions.

In the previously cited matter of *Gautam v. DeLuca*, (215 NJ Super 388, App. Div. 1987) the Appellate Division held that a loss by a former client is one that is "purely pecuniary." The court went on to say that the relationship between the client and the lawyer is one that is "predicated upon economic interests" (*id.*, page 401). Therefore, at least in New Jersey, under most circumstances emotional distress damages are not recoverable in a legal malpractice case. The New Jersey Court held that in order for a former client to collect damages for emotional distress, the conduct of the attorney must be egregious or there must be extraordinary circumstances. The Court went on to say that damages should be limited to economic loss, and also observed that even if damages were recoverable in legal malpractice actions for emotional distress, in the absence of "medical evidence establishing substantial bodily injury or severe demonstrative psychiatric sequelae," damages for emotional distress would not be recoverable (page 399). The Court concluded by noting that "aggravation, annoyance, and frustration, however real and justified, constitute unfortunate products of daily living" (page 400). Therefore, damages for emotional distress were disapproved and not allowed.

In legal malpractice cases, punitive damages are awarded for two purposes: to punish a defendant, and to deter similar future misconduct by other attorneys. In the event there is an intentional wrongdoing or gross negligence, some jurisdictions will justify an award of punitive damages. If it is found that the attorney willfully and wantonly disregarded a client's rights, a punitive damage award may be appropriate and allowed. In order for the plaintiff to recover punitive and/or exemplary damages, the conduct of the attorney must be wanton, reckless, or malicious. In the *Guatum v. DeLuca* matter, the Court could not find the type of conduct that would justify punitive damages, noting that there was no deliberate conduct or an omission by the attorney with a knowledge of high-degree of probability of harm and reckless indifference to the consequence (*id.,* page 401).

Legal fees are an element of damage that may be recoverable, along with expenses incurred, under certain circumstances. For example, consider an attorney who handles a real estate transaction on behalf of a client who is purchasing a home. The lawyer fails to secure the removal of a lien or fails to discover a lien which was placed on the property prior to closing. The new purchaser will now have to hire another attorney to have the lien removed. In that instance, the attorney's fees incurred in correcting the problem would be recoverable as an element of damage. However, in a contingency case, the attorney's fees in the legal malpractice case are generally not recoverable. For example, let's take the attorney who fails to file a claim within the applicable statute of limitations. That attorney is now sued by the former client. The client hires another lawyer who charges one-third of the recovery as a legal fee. This is what is commonly referred to as a "contingency fee." If the lawyer recovers for the client, the lawyer charges a fee of one-third of the recovery. The contingency is governed by state judicial mandate in most jurisdictions . In any event, those fees would not be recoverable. The reason they are not recoverable is that the client would have had to pay the same one-third contingency fee to the lawyer who was originally retained to handle the underlying case. The client has not suffered any additional legal fees.

To further clarify this example, let's say the client is injured in an automobile accident. The case is worth or has a value of $100,000. The client retains an attorney. The attorney fails to file a claim within the applicable statute of limitations. Had the attorney done so, the client would have recovered the $100,000 less costs and legal fees, which, let's say, would have left the client a net of $65,000. The client now has to hire a lawyer to sue the first lawyer for legal malpractice. The client's case still has that same value of $100,000 plus some consideration for interest and loss of use of the money. Let's assume for the purposes of this discussion that there are no damages recoverable for consequential losses, emotional distress, or punitive damages. When the second lawyer now sues the first lawyer, the case still has that same basic value of $100,000. If the second lawyer works on a contingency fee, he would then reduce the amount of the award by his costs and legal fees, leaving the client with the same basic net of $65,000 plus any consideration for interest and costs in connection with the litigation. Therefore, in the strict contingency case, the one-third recovery by the lawyer plus expenses is generally not recoverable.

There are a number of statutes which may apply to a lawsuit against a lawyer for legal malpractice. Many of these statutes would enable a client to sue for substantially more money than in traditional compensatory damage lawsuit. This would include statutes governing consumer fraud. It is not well established that the standard consumer fraud statutes apply to services provided by a lawyer. One would have to examine the legislation on a state-by-state basis to determine the applicability of the statutes to legal malpractice actions. If consumer fraud laws are applicable, the plaintiff or former client may be entitled to "treble damages," which are triple damages plus attorney's fees and costs in some jurisdictions. For example, in New Jersey, the relevant consumer fraud statute may be found at N.J.S.A. 56:8-1 et seq. If the attorney is deemed to have acted in an unconscionable commercial practice or deceptive fraud or false pretense; or did knowingly conceal certain facts, the attorney may be held liable for all these additional damages under New Jersey's Consumer Fraud Statute. There seems to be no reason why an attorney's conduct should not be governed by the ordinary consumer fraud statute. To date there is no reported decision on the point, however. ≡

X Lawyerproofing Your Case

SELECTING A LAWYER

WHEN A person needs an attorney, selection is frequently based on other people's recommendations. When a person seeks such recommendations, he may also want to consult other available sources, but these are limited. For example, the directory called *Martindale-Hubbell* lists attorneys by city and area of expertise. The difficulty with this directory, however, is that the information provided is self-serving. Each lawyer writes the description printed in *Martindale-Hubbell,* subject to the review, investigation, and editing by the staff of the publication. As a consequence, this resource provides very little real assistance to the client.

When a client seeks an attorney, I recommend that the client meet face to face with his or her prospective attorney to determine whether or not there's a mutual understanding and chemistry between them that would support a long-lasting relationship. Consider this: when a person purchases an automobile, the consumer first looks at several different models, and test-drives them before deciding which to buy. Yet when it comes to selecting a lawyer, most people hire a lawyer based on their first impression. The client should first ask the lawyer a number of questions, most of which are addressed in this chapter. The answers to such questions provide the ground rules for the attorney-client relationship. If a client is dissatisfied with the response from the attorney, the client should simply move on and find another attorney. Selecting a lawyer should be no different than any selection process involving a crucial decision. Compare it to the process of putting an addition on a home. Wouldn't the homeowner want to interview and get quotes or estimates from several different contractors? Getting to know the person you are hiring, whether for home improvements or legal help, is essential. Recommendations are often helpful, but they don't always mean that the person performing the service will be suitable for your particular job.

During the selection process, a client should also determine whether or not the lawyer specializes in a particular area of the law. Nothing should prevent a client from asking an attorney how many cases the attorney has handled like the one the client has. These questions, however, will not ensure that a lawyer will be completely responsive to the client's needs. Rather, the lawyer's reliability will be tested as the case progresses.

PARTICIPATION

CLIENTS RARELY take an active part in the handling of their cases. In most instances the client allows the attorney not only to make all decisions about the case, but also, by failing to demand that the attorney be responsive, allows the attorney to keep the client in the dark concerning the case's progress. I recommend that the client get a commitment from the attorney that the client will be an active participant in all phases of the case. The client should be given copies of all documents pertaining to the case, and should be informed of every aspect of the matter as it progresses. All decisions should be made jointly by the attorney and the client. Regrettably, most attorneys take offense at a client's active participation. On one of the "Morton Downey Jr. Shows" on which I argued in favor of filing lawsuits against lawyers for legal malpractice, there was a victim of medical malpractice on stage. This victim claimed that that attorney handling the medical malpractice case took it upon himself to reject a $600,000 offer from the defendants because the lawyer thought that the settlement figure was inadequate. The family, it was alleged, never knew of the $600,000 offer before the verdict, and it was only after the verdict that it was disclosed that a settlement offer had been made earlier in the case. Unfortunately, the jury returned a verdict of "zero" or "no cause" to this young boy and, as a consequence, the boy's family is attempting to seek a new trial through the appellate process. In the event that the boy receives no compensation for the medical aspects of his case, and if the attorney did, indeed, fail to communicate the offer, there certainly will be a suit filed against the attorney for legal malpractice.

SECOND OPINION

IN THE medical field we frequently hear of patients seeking out second opinions before surgery. Why shouldn't the same be true in the legal field? Since some legal decisions have the same impact as a scalpel has during surgery, a second opinion may be just as important in legal matters. Consider the example in which an attorney in a criminal case recommends that a defendant plead guilty. Right away, that client should go out and seek another legal opinion to determine whether or not the first attorney is rendering the proper advice. In many instances the first attorney is not correct. I was consulted in a case in which an attorney charged a client $100,000 for his defense. The lawyer persuaded the client to enter a plea of guilty, even though the client was innocent. The lawyer told the client that unless he pleaded guilty, his wife (the real wrongdoer) would immediately go to jail. At this point, the attorney assured his client that he would not go to jail if he pleaded guilty. Upon entering his plea of guilty, the client was carted out of the courtroom and led off to jail. Surely a second opinion would have avoided this result.

Sometimes a conflict of interest can sway a lawyer's behavior. For example, if an attorney is in immediate financial need, the attorney may seek an early settlement. The client, however, may wish to hold out for a substantial period of time in order to obtain a better result. This potential conflict could have been avoided with a second opinion and the client's more careful scrutiny of the lawyer's position.

We secure second opinions every day. Yet when it comes to hiring a lawyer to handle the purchase of a life-long dream, a house, we are content to allow a perfect stranger to determine the course of our future. For a mere consultation fee with another attorney, one can determine whether or not the first attorney is acting in an appropriate fashion.

Take another example of an attorney who is about to settle a personal injury case for a accident victim. That settlement is the only time the victim can seek compensation for the injury. For the attorney, however, there will certainly be other victims to be represented in the future. Obviously, the lawyer's attention to any one victim's case may not be nearly as focused as the client's. Therefore the client-victim should devote substantial time, energy, and resources to determine whether or not the attorney is truly acting in the client-victim's best interest.

COMMUNICATING THE TRUTH, THE WHOLE TRUTH, NOTHING BUT THE TRUTH.

I HAVE frequently said on televised debates that the attorneys who are most effective communicators in court are the least effective communicators with clients. Part of this problem stems from lawyers' taking on too much business. Another part of the problem is that attorneys do not tell the truth to their clients. Take, for example, an attorney who has an active trial practice. That attorney is frequently in court for the better part of the business day, usually between 9:00 A.M. and 4:30 P.M. When that attorney returns to the office, there are then numerous phone calls to be made and new clients to be interviewed. As a matter of priority, the attorney usually meets with the new clients before doing anything else. Rarely, if ever, does an attorney turn down new clients. As a consequence, the client who has had a case pending for a year will probably not receive a return phone call for hours, days, or longer. Since many lawyers do not limit the number of their cases, it is almost impossible for a good trial attorney to constantly communicate with all of his or her clients. There's just not enough time in the day to contact each client. As a result, most clients are left in the dark about the day-to-day progress of their cases. The real problem lies in lawyers who fail or refuse to communicate to their clients at all. In most malpractice cases there is a complete lack of communication between lawyer and client.

I have a few recommendations about this problem. First, the lawyer should consider limiting the number of clients and cases handled. If this suggestion seems offensive or impractical, consider the consequences of a lawyer's taking on too many cases. The lawyer cannot give the proper attention to each case. Undoubtedly, that lawyer will eventually be guilty of some kind of legal malpractice, whether by missing a statute of limitations or forgetting to tell a client that an important decision needs to be made. To me, this is the price clients pay for their lawyers' taking on far too many cases.

I also advise attorneys to let their clients know their availability right up front. Although the attorney does not want to lose a new client, the attorney should be fair in his estimation of time available for the handling of a new client's matters. The same may be said of an attorney providing a client with expectations about the outcome of a particular case. An attorney who wants to please a client finds it much easier to agree with the client concerning the client's expectations. During their first meeting or certainly as soon as the attorney has had an opportunity to assess a particular matter, the attorney should advise the client of the realistic prospects for recovery and the costs involved in the case. Such candor by lawyers would help reduce legal malpractice suits started by clients who later have their high expectations and false hopes (and pocketbooks) crushed by the hard realities of the courtroom.

FEES & RETAINER AGREEMENTS

LEGAL FEES are out of control! Most people in America cannot afford to hire a lawyer. For the very poor, in many cases, free legal services are available. On the other hand, the very rich have no difficulty in hiring lawyers. For the majority of Americans, however, legal fees put lawyers out of reach. What's worse, it is generally not until after the client has already retained the lawyer that the fees are discussed. As I mentioned before, there always should be a retainer agreement. The retainer agreement should specifically state the nature and the extent of the legal fees, what the client should expect in terms of future billings, and how these monies are to be collected. The retainer agreement should also establish whether a lawyer will work for an hourly rate, a contingency rate, or a combination of both. In a contingency case, an attorney is paid a percentage of the recovery. In contingency retainers there are also questions about handling appeals and the payment of appeal costs. Who pays these expenses? Will these considerations influence the lawyer's handling of the case? Also, When are these fees payable? Many of these issues usually concealed from the clients until the bill arrives in the mail.

Nothing provokes more legal malpractice lawsuits than fee disputes. Suing the lawyer often seems to be the only way a client can combat an attorney who is overcharging or who is charging a fee that is inconsistent with the client's prior expectations. There are, however, alternative administrative remedies that are time-consuming and sometimes costly to the client. One such remedy is the fee arbitration committee. These committees decide what fee (if any) an attorney is entitled to when there is a dispute between a lawyer and client. In my own experience, I have found that most clients are wary and suspect these proceedings, since they are run primarily by lawyers for lawyers. Also, these proceedings are often binding upon the parties, which means they may prevent someone from ever bringing a malpractice lawsuit against the lawyer.

I have talked to clients throughout the United States who complain about legal fees when their relationship with the lawyer terminates. For example, if the client becomes frustrated with his or her lawyer and fires that lawyer or, on the other hand, if the lawyer seeks to get out of handling a case after the lawyer has agreed to represent the client, there will be questions about payment. These situations will present problems to the client and the lawyer if such matters are not covered in the retainer agreement.

A complete retainer agreement should also provide for what we call an "engagement letter." This document states what the attorney's obligations are and what the client's obligations are. Lacking in almost all of these engagement letters are the attorney's duties regarding communication — returning telephone calls and providing copies of all pertinent papers and documents. The engagement letter should also contain a provision for declining a case right from the beginning. This means that when the attorney decides not to handle a case, the attorney should send a letter declining the case and informing the client of his or her right from this point forward. This letter should also advise the client of any applicable statute of limitations.

DOCKET CONTROL & DIARY

LAWYERS ALWAYS work under severe time limitations. This is obvious when one analyzes the American Bar Association's *Profile on Legal Malpractice.* This report states that a sizeable number of claims are filed against lawyers for failure to abide by strict time limits. Either the lawyer does not know these limits or knows them but, nevertheless, fails to meet them. Consider a personal injury case. In such cases, if the defendant is a governmental subdivision, a special notice of intent to file a claim, in many states, must be sent to the proper government subdivision within a relatively short time. For example if the injury happened in New Jersey, a notice must be forwarded to the appropriate government subdivision within ninety days from the time of the accident. The client may not be able to recover for injuries unless that ninety-day notice of intention to make a claim is actually filed. While there are a few exceptions that allow a client to file a late notice, in most instances the notice requirement must be satisfied in order for the client to have a case against the entity. If the lawyer doesn't file the notice, or files it too late, the victim may find that he or she has no case.

There are time limitations involved in almost every kind of lawsuit. That is, each lawsuit must be brought on or before the applicable statute would forever bar the bringing of the particular claim. While a discovery period may be available to extend some statutes of limitations, there are still fixed time limits within which the attorney is required to perform certain acts. There are also certain procedures that an attorney must follow in handling a case. For example, consider discovery. "Discovery" is a litigation procedure that allows each side to see what the other side's case is all about. Discovery may include interrogatories, depositions, requests for admissions, and so on. "Interrogatories" are written questions given by one attorney to the other, which the client must answer. "Depositions" are sworn statements taken under oath, as though they were made in the actual courtroom, although they are not.

In each of these proceedings there are strict time limits for serving, answering, or otherwise fulfilling these matters. Applications can be made to the court to extend or modify these time limits. Without such an application, however, the client may be prejudiced by either dismissal of the case or suppression of a defense. There may be other sanctions that would deprive the client of an opportunity to have the case heard. When an attorney fails to work within these time limits, irreparable damage may be done to the client's case.

Time limits mark the entire life of a legal case. They are present from the minute a complaint is filed or a case begins, to the final minutes in the litigation. Many lawyers do not abide by these strict, but necessary, time limits. As a consequence, these lawyers are faced with telling their clients that they overlooked or missed a critical deadline. Regrettably, attorneys opt not to tell the truth, but to misrepresent the status of the case to the client. For this reason, I recommend that every client should maintain a diary and should know the time limitations applicable to the case. The diary should include the dates and times of any meetings, decisions, time limitations, and copies of papers filed with the clerk of the court related to the client, the lawyer, and the case. This way a client can monitor the lawyer's actions. For example, if an attorney has sixty days to answer interrogatories, the client should be aware of that fact from the outset. Once the client knows these time limitations, the client can then direct the attorney to follow up, especially if time is running out.

Another method of checking on an attorney when the attorney is not fully candid is to go directly to the courthouse and check the file itself. In many cases I advise clients to learn how to find the truth about their cases by going to the court file. A candid, communicative lawyer would certainly save a client from the anguish and emotional distress of such a trip to the courthouse.

REFERRAL & SPECIALIZATION

IN MANY jurisdictions, the state supreme court certifies certain attorneys as being specialists in civil or criminal trial practice. Whether or not the attorney has expertise in the area of a specific case is questionable. Let's say, for example, that a client is able to find an attorney to handle a legal malpractice case against another lawyer. Let's also assume that the attorney is a certified civil trial attorney, but has never handled a legal malpractice matter before. Obviously, the attorney is not going to be well versed in handling this particular case, even though the attorney has been in the courtroom many times and is certified as a civil trial attorney. Should the client ask the lawyer to refer the case to a specialist? To answer this question, let's briefly look at the practice of law in general.

A general practitioner, one who practices all aspects of general law, will not be equipped to handle a case involving a specialized area of the law. Today no lawyer can keep up with the growing body of knowledge encompassing all aspects of the practice of law. A client should question a lawyer at length regarding the lawyer's background and experience in handling the client's type of case.

Another question a client should ask is whether or not the lawyer attends continuing legal education programs in the lawyer's specialty. These seminars are actually how-to lectures given by experts in various aspects to the law. Lawyers attend these seminars to learn how to handle particular matters, to brush up on new developments in a particular area, or to gain certification in a specialized area of the law. Despite the fact these sessions are open to the general public, very few lawyers encourage their clients to attend. Although it is an excellent way for clients to educate themselves about their own cases, lawyers attempt to monopolize the practice of law and usually exclude their clients from knowledge of these seminars. Clients, however, can directly benefit from these seminars, and I can think of no better way for clients to learn about legal procedures and the details involved in their own lawsuits than by taking the time to attend a relevant program.

I have served as both a moderator and lecturer at legal malpractice seminars. They were attended only by lawyers. I can only recommend that more non-lawyers attend so that they as well as the attorneys better understand how the process works.

CONFLICT OF INTEREST

MOST CONFLICTS of interest occur for one of three reasons: greed; a failure by law firms to have a system that will uncover conflicts of interest; and lawyers acting as partners or co-investors with clients, either as part owners of businesses with or as officers or directors of their client's business enterprises. These situations are prevalent because lawyers are notorious for representing both sides of an issue. For example, when there is a sale and purchase of a business, one lawyer frequently represents both the buyer and seller. A lawyer should represent only one side of the transaction. When the lawyer represents both sides, disclaimers must be made to either one or both of the parties involved. Regrettably, this isn't always the case. Let's take, for example, the attorney who represents both the buyer and the seller in the sale of a business. The seller agrees to accept a promissory note from the buyer as part of the transaction. Keep in mind that the attorney represents both the buyer and the seller and prepares all of the paperwork and documents in connection with this transaction. If the buyer is later unable to pay the seller what is owed for the business, there is a default. If the attorney was not in a conflict of interest before, he certainly is now. Although I take the position that there is an automatic conflict of interest when the attorney represents both sides of the transaction, in this case the conflict is clear. In many cases like this, the attorney will seek to give advice to both the buyer and seller after a default. Now the seller finds out that the attorney was negligent in drafting the documents right from the beginning. The seller also discovers that the lawyer now represents the buyer in connection with all of the buyer's business dealings. I see this situation regularly. Why is it so common? Because of the lawyers' greed. Lawyers should never get involved in this type of conflict of interest, particularly since ethical rules prohibit this type of dual representation. A lawyer should never be permitted to represent both sides of a transaction or, alternatively, to represent a former client who has interests adverse to his present client. The information that the lawyer gained in trust will certainly damage the former client.

A similar situation occurs when a criminal defense attorney represents more than one defendant in a criminal trial. I always recommend that a lawyer represent only one defendant in a criminal case. Yet criminal lawyers all too often represent more than one defendant in cases where there are multiple defendants. I see many instances where the criminal defendant later claims that the lawyer favored another defendant for any one of a variety of reasons. The lawyer is automatically exposed to a claim of conflict of interest under these circumstances. Why do they do it? Greed.

Another conflict of interest situation involves law firms that are negligent in keeping a cross-referenced list of clients. Partly because of the pressure to act as a business, law firms often bend the rules, allowing associates and partners to take on clients despite obvious conflicts of interest.

When an attorney serves as a corporate director, or officer, or partner with the client, or is a part owner of the client's business, conflicts of interest will undoubtedly appear in time. These conflicts of interest become more complex when the business either has had or is about to have dealings with another business represented by the attorney's own law firm. An attorney should not be a partner with a client or participate with the client in a business venture unless the client has gotten independent legal advice and there has been a full and absolute disclosure of all of the facts and circumstances surrounding the business relationship as well as any potential conflict of interest.

LAWYERS' ABUSE OF THE LEGAL PROCESS

WHEN LAWYERS engage in one-upmanship, it inevitably results in losses to the client. Lawyers are notorious for abusing the system by trying to outmaneuver their opponents, often at the expense of the clients. Certainly a lawyer should aggressively advocate the client's interests, but in most instances, lawyers attempt to beat up on one another through the use of unnecessary litigation. This results in both inordinate delays in the legal process and astronomical legal expenses. At present there are rules imposed on the federal and state levels that outline a lawyer's responsibilities with regard to filing complaints, answering complaints, filing motions, and directing any other process in connection with a legal proceeding. If a lawyer is overzealous or abuses the system, the lawyer may be sanctioned by the court or held responsible for fees and expenses that the other side incurred.

States now allow for separate causes of action to be filed against attorneys by any party who is aggrieved by the attorney's misconduct. These new causes of action allow suits for damages to be filed against lawyers who abuse the system or who seek to harass, intimidate, or coerce members of the opposing side. Lawyers frequently commit such offenses by filing frivolous motions with the court or by filing unnecessary discovery requests, requiring the disadvantaged party to pay unnecessary legal fees and costs to fight these motions.

The courts have grown tired of this unnecessary litigation. There is now a movement to allow the party subjected to these expenses to file lawsuits against the abusive attorneys. While our country's system has not adopted the European view, which allows legal fees to be awarded to the winning party, at least the system recognizes in some cases that lawyers who abuse the system may be responsible for damages. The courts and legislatures have not gone far enough, however. It is now time for severe sanctions to be imposed on lawyers who abuse the system. The argument against the imposition of sanctions is that we do not want to discourage people from using the legal system. Some argue that these sanctions have a chilling effect upon the individual's right to use the legal system. I say that is nonsense. I have witnessed, time and time again, the abuse of the legal system by lawyers. It's about time lawyers pay for this abuse.

A question that arises concerns the client who is held responsible for damages due to a lawyer's misconduct. Must the client sue the lawyer for malpractice in order to recover for these damages?

For example, a client came to me for advice after his attorney stood at the client's public hearing and made defamatory remarks and threatened the adverse party. Then the adverse party filed a lawsuit against both the attorney and the client because of the attorney's inappropriate actions. The charge was that the attorney had intentionally intimidated the other side with the threatening remarks. The client suffered by having to pay substantial legal expenses to defend himself. Although the remarks eventually were determined to be privileged, and therefore not actionable, the client was forced to spend a considerable amount of money to defend himself. At no time did the attorney offer to pay, contribute, or absorb the costs. In fact, the attorney relied on the client to pay for all the legal expenses in connection with the defense. It's this type of misconduct that needs to be addressed and remedied. In such cases, it's obvious that our legal system is out of control because of overzealous lawyers who abuse the system. It is time to look at some possible remedies. ≡

XI Remedies to the Legal Malpractice Crisis

THE LEGAL MALPRACTICE INSTITUTE

WHEN I created the Legal Malpractice Institute, I anticipated widespread public dissatisfaction with attorneys. I created the Legal Malpractice Institute to not only publish this book, but to provide public consulting and seminars to advise people of their right to sue lawyers. Since beginning these efforts, I have found myself overwhelmed with phone calls from people who are desperate to find lawyers who will sue other lawyers for legal malpractice. This has led me to devote my efforts to establishing a nationwide network of lawyers who are willing to handle lawsuits against other lawyers. I have already discussed this issue with a limited number of lawyers. I usually find that lawyers are unwilling to sue other lawyers, except under a very limited set of circumstances. These circumstances include that the case should have "substantial exposure." That is, there must be a lot of money involved. When there is a lot of money involved and liability is clear (when the lawyer is guilty of gross malpractice), lawyers will sue other lawyers. Another consideration frequently expressed is that there has to be malpractice insurance to cover the loss. If the law firm or the lawyer is uninsured, chances are that it will be a real problem to find a lawyer to handle the legal malpractice case. I know this from first-hand knowledge and experience.

After one of my television appearances discussing legal malpractice, I received some two thousand phone calls from people who wanted to make legal malpractice claims against lawyers. I tried in vain to associate myself with another law firm or other lawyers to handle these cases. The law firms, however, responded by saying that they were not interested or that they would handle these types of cases only under certain circumstances. These conditions included that the errant lawyer was insured for the loss and that the lawyer's conduct was so egregious that a finding of malpractice would be inevitable. If there was questionable liability, the lawyer or firm would refuse to become involved. Because of these negative responses from law firms, I contacted a management consulting search firm to see if they could find a law firm that would be interested in working with me on these cases. The management consulting firm discovered that no law firms were interested. So, I had no choice but to pursue this mission on my own. Finally I found a law firm with which to associate as of counsel. We will now handle legal malpractice cases.

ARBITRATION & ALTERNATIVE DISPUTE RESOLUTIONS

WE MUST recognize that our present system does not work, primarily because the majority of Americans have insufficient access to the legal system. Lawyers are too costly and the system is too slow. One remedy may be to eliminate the monopoly lawyers hold, by allowing more cases to be resolved through arbitration and alternative dispute resolution systems. Lawyers and non-lawyers can both participate in the arbitration process. In arbitration, an unbiased third party resolves disputes, thus eliminating lengthy, costly court sessions. In arbitration, the rules of evidence are relaxed or suspended to allow the lay person and the attorney equal opportunity to argue their points. Without the rigid restrictions of the court system (which favors lawyers), both sides can be judged fairly. Alternative dispute resolution includes mediation and other methods of resolving disputes that avoid going through the legal system. All of these solutions would provide for a less expensive and, probably, more expeditious resolution of differences between people. This is important, because the majority of people can today no longer afford to fight out their differences with expensive hired guns. Legal abuses would be minimized by a system that encourages resolution of disputes instead of the creation of more disputes.

RISK MANAGEMENT & EARLY INTERVENTION

MOST LAWYERS have little or no risk management experience related to legal malpractice. Seminars on avoiding legal malpractice claims are sparsely attended by lawyers, especially those lawyers at the highest risk of incurring a lawsuit. In fact, during the course of one lecture I attended, a speaker said he felt as if he was giving a lecture to the converted. He meant that those lawyers concerned with learning how to avoid committing legal malpractice were the very lawyers who do not need such a lecture. Too often, it is those lawyers who express no concern or interest in the subject who should (but do not) attend these seminars. The problem is how to encourage these lawyers to participate. One way is through the insurance system. Making it economically rewarding for an attorney to learn how to avoid malpractice would undoubtedly encourage the lawyer to do so. One incentive could be reduced premiums for lawyers who have been free from negligence claims or who have attended some risk management seminars.

When I say "risk management," I mean educational programs backed by a compilation of loss-ratio statistics, to keep legal malpractice at a minimum. This is already done in automobile insurance. If a driver attends driver education programs, or has no points on his license for a number of years, the driver is entitled to a reduction in the premium. Why isn't the same practice applied to lawyers? Rarely, if ever, do insurance companies engage in effective risk management. There are too few insurance companies that encourage lawyers to participate in these worthwhile programs to improve themselves. Although insurance companies have the first opportunity to see where attorneys err, they fail to take advantage of this opportunity. They should either teach lawyers how not to practice law, thus discouraging legal malpractice claims, or they should positively emphasize the proper way to practice, also reducing legal malpractice claims.

Another example of risk management involves an insurance application form that is completed by attorneys. All attorneys must check off whether they have a docket control and diary system. The insurance companies, however, do not check on these systems. If the insurance companies did, the lawyers would be forced to engage in risk management by implementing controls. At the present time, lawyers have no incentive to implement controls.

Another possible remedy involves early intervention or, as some refer to it, "claims repair." The attorney who errs may have that mistake salvaged and the case restored back to its original condition if there is early intervention. The insurance companies should encourage early intervention. Instead, they ignore it. I recently engaged in an experimental case on behalf of an insurance company. In that case, an attorney suffered from an alcohol-related problem. The insurance company was persuaded to engage in early intervention, allowing us to review all of the attorney's files and to try to create solutions for any problem files. While the experiment was a success, the insurance company vowed not to try it again. It seems as though no one is interested in aggressive responses to the malpractice problem. When there is a problem in legal malpractice, it cannot be ignored. Left alone, a lawyer's problem files will get out of control at the direct expense of his or her clients.

ADMINISTRATIVE PROCEEDINGS FOR COMPLAINTS

THERE IS a variety of administrative committees which already exist and which have been designed to redress attorney misconduct. Most notable among these are the ethics committees. The procedures before these committees, however, are generally complex and involve prosecution of an attorney for unethical conduct. Unfortunately, this system does not award compensation to the victim. The victim may get a pound of flesh by prosecuting the attorney before his peers, but this does not compensate the victim for his or her losses. The ethics system, moreover, is run mostly by those who participate in the legal system. The only purpose of the ethics committee is to make a judgment of the lawyer's conduct. The fact of the matter is, the victim is not served by this ethics proceeding. Although the attorneys engaged in this process devote considerable time and effort toward prosecuting unethical lawyers, they deal with only a very small percentage of the overall population of lawyers. Reliance upon these proceedings to weed out bad lawyers is misplaced. I often argue that the focus must be on the manner in which lawyers practice law, and not so much on those few attorneys who are ultimately expelled or suspended from the practice of law. Victims are simply not compensated by the disciplinary system, both because too few lawyers are disbarred or suspended and because the system drags on while the victim is without effective compensation.

There are other administrative agencies, like client security funds, through which claims may be processed against lawyers who steal from clients. Again, however, we are dealing with only a small percentage of lawyers. While these agencies serve a vital function, because of their very limited purposes they service only a small fraction of the clients who are harmed by lawyers' misconduct.

There are also fee arbitration committees which may be asked to resolve fee disputes between clients and lawyers. Most cases of lawyers' negligence result in substantial damages to clients, and fee dispute resolution may, therefore, be of only minor concern. Clients must, moreover, be mindful of the fact that once they invoke the fee dispute resolution process, they may be barred from instituting a separate claim for legal malpractice.

There are also bar association committees that may help resolve some problems. I have served on both local and state bar association committees designed to assist impaired lawyers. In New Jersey, for example, there is no really effective provision for assisting lawyers who are physically or emotionally impaired. Clearly, there is a need for clients to be protected when their attorney is impaired by drugs or alcohol or is otherwise incapable of practicing as a consequence of stress, emotional, or other disabilities. We know that one out of every six persons suffers from some form of impairment, be it drug or alcohol abuse or some other disability. Committees must be established to deal with this situation; the client must be protected and assured that there will be an orderly transition of the file or case when it is determined that the attorney, for whatever reason, is not longer able to attend to that file.

SUE ALL THE LAWYERS

WHEN LAWYERS were dissatisfied with the doctors' actions and the ways they conducted their practices, they began to sue those doctors for medical malpractice. When lawyers became dissatisfied with the phrase "caveat emptor" (Let the Buyer Beware), they began to sue the manufacturers and distributors of dangerous products. Medical malpractice and product liability lawsuits have changed industries and professions. We, now as lawyers, must begin to look to our own profession. Changes are obviously needed in how lawyers practice law. Malpractice suits seem to be the only effective means available today to motivate the legal profession into changing the way lawyers do business. Although sanctions have been imposed against lawyers who are overzealous or who act in bad faith, these sanctions have been neither effective in dealing with errant lawyers nor have these sanctions compensated the victims of legal malpractice.

Legal malpractice, today, is simply out of control. It is when lawyers begin to pay out of their own pocketbooks for damages, that there will be a change. Only then, when the lawyers have to reach into their own pockets to pay for the mental anguish and emotional distress to their victims of legal malpractice, will the lawyers start changing the system from within.

When lawyers themselves become the targets of the protracted lawsuit, the legal profession will finally realize the tyranny under which clients have had to suffer. It is then and only then that lawyers will wake up and realize that they have adversely affected the lives of many people by the way they do business. When the lawyer is finally sued, the lawyer is then subjected to the same system that enslaves the rest of us when we are the victims of legal malpractice. By suing lawyers for legal negligence and malpractice, clients will then finally be compensated for the errant conduct of their attorneys. For the benefit of both the legal profession as well as the public at large, victims must reach out and develop a network of lawyers willing to take on these cases, even if they are few in number. By their very success these lawyers will wake up the rest of the legal profession to their responsibility to their clients. Only after lawyers are sued will we see a change. The legal malpractice crisis is with us. The question is — Will we let it stay or will we do something about it? I now devote almost my entire practice to suing lawyers. I am doing something about it. Join me. Sue the lawyers! ≡

XII Form Samples

SAMPLE COMPLAINT/ LAWSUIT FOR LEGAL MALPRACTICE

Good Guy, Esq.
123 Justice Lane
Anywhere, New Jersey 00000
(201)123-4567
Attorney for Plaintiff

SUPERIOR COURT OF NEW JERSEY
LAW DIVISION — MORRIS COUNTY
DOCKET NO. A-1234-89

Ima Victim
 	
                    Plaintiff
                         vs.
Malpractice Lawyer and
XYZ Law Firm, Jointly, Severally,
and in the Alternative
                    Defendants
	Civil Action
	
	COMPLAINT FOR
	LEGAL MALPRACTICE

The Plaintiff, Ima Victim, residing at 1 Poor House Road in the City of Morristown, County of Morris, as and for his Complaint against Malpractice Lawyer and XYZ Law Firm, Jointly, Severally, and in the Alternative, says:

161

FIRST COUNT

1. The Plaintiff, Ima Victim, at all times hereinafter mentioned, resides at 1 Poor House Road, Morristown, New Jersey.

2. At all times hereinafter mentioned, Malpractice Lawyer was an attorney at law of the State of New Jersey.

3. At all times hereinafter mentioned, XYZ Law Firm was either a professional corporation, a partnership, or an entity formed to do business in the State of New Jersey and engaged in the practice of law.

4. At all times hereinafter mentioned, Malpractice Lawyer was an agent, employee, shareholder, partner, and/or independent contractor, engaged in a relationship with XYZ Law Firm, a Professional Corporation, in the practice of law.

5. Malpractice Lawyer was admitted to the practice of law in the State of New Jersey on 1st day of January 1908 and has had his principal place of business at in the City of Morristown, County of Morris, New Jersey.

6. XYZ Law Firm has a principal place of business at Get Rich Quick Road, in the City of Morristown, County of Morris, New Jersey.

7. Ima Victim was injured in an accident on 1st day of January 1985. As a direct and proximate result of this accident, Ima Victim sustained severe injuries due to the vehicle which was owned and negligently operated by John Wrongdoer. Ima Victim was not negligent in connection with the operation of his vehicle.

8. Ima Victim, on 2nd day of January 1985, visited the offices of Malpractice Lawyer and XYZ Law Firm to have his interests represented in connection with the accident of 1st day of January 1985.

9. On or about May 1985, XYZ Law Firm and Malpractice Lawyer entered into a Retainer Agreement with Ima Victim wherein XYZ Law Firm and Malpractice Lawyer were retained to represent Ima Victim in connection with the accident that occurred on 1st day of January 1985.

10. Malpractice Lawyer had the duty to exercise the knowledge, skill,

ability and devotion ordinarily possessed and employed by members of the legal profession similarly situated, in connection with the discharge of his responsibilities to Ima Victim, and to utilize reasonable care and prudence in connection with those responsibilities.

11. XYZ Law Firm had the duty to exercise the knowledge, skill, ability and devotion ordinarily possessed and employed by members of the legal profession, in connection with the discharge of its responsibilities to Ima Victim.

12. Malpractice Lawyer and XYZ Law Firm failed to institute a suit on behalf of Ima Victim within the applicable statute of limitations. As a direct and proximate result, Ima Victim is forever barred from instituting a lawsuit for injuries sustained in the accident of January 1, 1985.

13. Ima Victim made repeated telephone calls to Malpractice Lawyer and to XYZ Law Firm to learn the status of his matter. Malpractice Lawyer and the XYZ Law Firm failed to disclose to Ima Victim that his lawsuit was not instituted within the applicable statute of limitations. XYZ Law Firm and Malpractice Lawyer, moreover, fraudulently concealed their negligence and misrepresented the status of this case to Ima Victim.

14. Malpractice Lawyer breached his duty to Ima Victim by his failure to exercise the knowledge, skill, ability, and devotion ordinarily possessed and employed by members of the legal profession similarly situated, in connection with the discharge of his responsibilities to Ima Victim, and breached his duty to utilize reasonable care and prudence in connection with those responsibilities.

15. XYZ Law Firm breached its duty to Ima Victim by its failure to exercise the knowledge, skill, ability, and devotion ordinarily possessed and employed by members of the legal profession similarly situated, in connection with the discharge of its responsibilities to Plaintiff, Ima Victim, and breached its duty to utilize reasonable care and prudence in connection with those responsibilities.

16. As a direct and proximate result of the negligence jointly, severally, and in the alternative of XYZ Law Firm and Malpractice Lawyer, Ima Victim was caused to suffer damages.

WHEREFORE, the Plaintiff, Ima Victim, demands judgment against Malpractice Lawyer and XYZ Law Firm, jointly, severally and in the alternative for:

A. Compensatory Damages;
B. Interest;
C. Costs of suit;
D. Attorneys fees; and
E. Any other relief the Court may deem equitable and just.

SECOND COUNT

1. Ima Victim repeats and reiterates each and every paragraph of the First Count of the Complaint as though the same were set forth at length herein.

2. XYZ Law Firm and Malpractice Lawyer breached their respective duties owed to Ima Victim by committing legal malpractice.

3. As a direct and proximate result of the legal malpractice of XYZ Law Firm and Malpractice Lawyer, Ima Victim was caused to suffer damages.

WHEREFORE, Plaintiff, Ima Victim demands judgment at Malpractice Lawyer and XYZ Law Firm, jointly, severally and in the alternative for:

A. Compensatory damages;
B. Interest;
C. Cost of suit;
D. Attorneys fees; and
E. Any other relief the Court may deem equitable and just.

THIRD COUNT

1. Ima Victim repeats and reiterates each and every paragraph of the First and Second Counts of the Complaint as though the same were set forth at length herein.

2. The conduct of XYZ Law Firm and Malpractice Lawyer, was professionally negligent, careless, and constituted a breach of the fiduciary relationship which each had with Ima Victim.

3. As a direct and proximate result of the professional negligence, carelessness, and breach of fiduciary relationship, Ima Victim was damaged.

4. XYZ Law Firm and Malpractice Lawyer violated the *Rules of Professional Conduct* [be specific] in connection with the discharge of their responsibilities and duties owed to Ima Victim.

WHEREFORE, Plaintiff, Ima Victim, demands judgment against XYZ Law Firm and Malpractice Lawyer, jointly, severally, and in the alternative, for:

    A. Damages;
    B. Interest;
    C. Costs of suit;
    D. Attorneys fees;
    E. Punitive Damages; and
    F. Any other relief the Court may deem equitable and just.

FOURTH COUNT

1. Ima Victim repeats and reiterates each and every paragraph of the First, Second, and Third Counts of the Complaint as though the same were set forth at length herein.

2. The conduct of XYZ Law Firm and Malpractice Lawyer constituted misrepresentation, intentional and/or negligent misrepresentation.

3. As a direct and proximate result of the intentional and/or negligent misrepresentation, Ima Victim was damaged.

4. XYZ Law Firm and Malpractice Lawyer violated the *Rules of Professional Conduct* [be specific] in connection with the discharge of their responsibilities and duties owed to Ima Victim.

WHEREFORE, Plaintiff, Ima Victim, demands judgment against XYZ Law Firm and Malpractice Lawyer, jointly, severally, and in the alternative, for:

    A. Compensatory Damages;
    B. Punitive Damages;
    C. Interest;

D. Costs of suit;
E. Attorneys fees; and
F. Any other relief the Court may deem equitable an just.

FIFTH COUNT

1. Ima Victim repeats and reiterates each and every paragraph of the First, Second, Third, and Fourth Counts of the Complaint as though the same were set forth at length herein.

2. The conduct of XYZ Law Firm and Malpractice Lawyer constituted a breach of contract, oral, implied, and/or express as to Ima Victim.

3. As a direct and proximate result of the breach of the oral, implied, and/or express contract and their respective duties owed to Ima Victim, XYZ Law Firm and Malpractice Lawyer caused Ima Victim to suffer damages, including special damages.

WHEREFORE, Plaintiff, Ima Victim demands judgment against Malpractice Lawyer and XYZ Law Firm, jointly, severally, and in the alternative, for:

A. Compensatory Damages;
B. Punitive Damages;
C. Interest;
D. Costs of suit;
E. Attorneys fees;
F. Consequential Damages; and
G. Any other relief the Court may deem equitable and just.

SIXTH COUNT

1. Ima Victim repeats and reiterates each and every paragraph of the First, Second, Third, Fourth, and Fifth Counts of the Complaint as though the same were set forth in length herein.

2. The conduct of XYZ Law Firm and Malpractice Lawyer constituted a breach of warranties, both implied and express, and a breach of the implied covenant of good faith and fair dealing.

3. As a direct and proximate result of the breach of warranties, both expressed and implied, and breach of the implied covenant of good faith and fair dealing, by XYZ Law Firm and Malpractice Lawyer, Ima Victim was caused to suffer damages, including special damages.

WHEREFORE, Plaintiff, Ima Victim demands judgment against Malpractice Lawyer and XYZ Law Firm, jointly, severally, and in the alternative, for:

A. Compensatory Damages;
B. Punitive Damages;
C. Interest;
D. Costs of suit;
E. Attorneys fees;
F. Special and Consequential Damages; and
G. Any other relief the Court may deem equitable and just.

SEVENTH COUNT

1. Plaintiff, Ima Victim, repeats and reiterates each and every paragraph of the First, Second, Third, Fourth, Fifth, and Sixth Counts of the Complaint as though the same were set forth in length herein.

2. The conduct of Malpractice Lawyer and XYZ Law Firm was willful, wanton, reckless and malicious, and their conduct constituted conscious and intentional wrongdoing, causing Ima Victim to suffer damages.

WHEREFORE, Plaintiff, Ima Victim demands judgment against Malpractice Lawyer and XYZ Law Firm, jointly, severally, and in the alternative, for:

A. Compensatory Damages;
B. Punitive Damages;
C. Interest;
D. Costs of suit;
E. Attorneys fees;
F. Special and Consequential Damages; and
G. Any other relief the Court may deem equitable and just.

EIGHTH COUNT

[Where Applicable, Insert Consumer Fraud Statutes]

1. Ima Victim repeats and reiterates each and every paragraph of the First, Second, Third, Fourth, Fifth, Sixth, and Seventh Counts of the Complaint as though the same were set forth in length herein.

2. At all times mentioned herein in this pleading and subsequent thereto, the Defendants, XYZ Law Firm and Malpractice Lawyer, did advertise and did otherwise hold themselves out as persons engaged in the business of providing to the public legal services to induce persons such as Ima Victim to retain their services.

3. XYZ Law Firm and Malpractice Lawyer did act unlawfully in rendering or failing to render the services; did act, use, or employ certain unconscionable commercial practices, deceptive frauds, false pretenses, false promises, misrepresentations, or did knowingly conceal, suppress, or omit certain material facts with intent that Ima Victim would rely upon such concealment, suppression, or omission in connection with the sale or advertisement or otherwise holding out of services, in violation of the New Jersey Consumer Fraud Act, N.J.S.A. 56:8-1 et seq.

4. As a direct and proximate result and consequence of the use or employment by the Defendants, Malpractice Lawyer and XYZ Law Firm, jointly, severally, and in the alternative, of the above methods, acts, and practices, Ima Victim did rely upon those actions of the Defendants, Malpractice Lawyer and XYZ Law Firm, and did suffer loss of monies or property.

WHEREFORE, Plaintiff, Ima Victim demands judgment against Malpractice Lawyer and XYZ Law Firm, jointly, severally, and in the alternative, for:

A. Compensatory Damages;
B. Punitive Damages;
C. Treble Damages;
D. Attorneys Fees;
E. Costs of suit;
F. Interest; and
G. Any other relief the Court may deem equitable and just.

NINTH COUNT

1. Plaintiff, Ima Victim, repeats and reiterates each and every paragraph of the First, Second, Third, Fourth, Fifth, Sixth, Seventh, and Eighth Counts of the Complaint as though the same were set forth at length herein.

2. The conduct of XYZ Law Firm and Malpractice Lawyer, jointly, severally, and in the alternative, was egregious towards Ima Victim in that the Defendants, XYZ Law Firm and Malpractice Lawyer, did act in a willful, wanton, reckless, and malicious manner and were conscious wrongdoers against Ima Victim.

3. Further, XYZ Law Firm and Malpractice Lawyer, jointly, severally, and in the alternative, did act deliberately with knowledge of a high degree of probability of harm to Ima Victim and did act with reckless indifference to the consequences of their conduct and harm to be suffered by Ima Victim.

4. As a direct and proximate result of the conduct of the XYZ Law Firm and Malpractice Lawyer, jointly, severally, and in the alternative, Ima Victim suffered damages.

WHEREFORE, Plaintiff, Ima Victim demands judgment against XYZ Law Firm and Malpractice Lawyer, jointly, severally, and in the alternative, for:

    A. Compensatory Damages;
    B. Punitive Damages;
    C. Interest;
    D. Cost of suit;
    E. Attorneys fees;
    F. Damages for emotional distress and mental anguish;
    G. Special Damages; and
    H. Any other relief the Court may deem equitable and just.

TENTH COUNT

1. Plaintiff, Ima Victim, repeats and reiterates each and every paragraph of the First, Second, Third, Fourth, Fifth, Sixth, Seventh, Eighth, and Ninth Counts of the Complaint as though the same were set forth at length herein.

2. The XYZ Law Firm and Malpractice Lawyer breached their respective duties owed to Ima Victim and acted in a wanton and willful disregard of the rights of Ima Victim.

3. As a direct and proximate result of the wanton and willful conduct on part of the Defendants, the Plaintiff suffered damages.

4. The conduct of XYZ Law Firm and Malpractice Lawyer was egregious, and the Defendants acted in a willful, wanton, reckless, or malicious manner and were consciously wrongdoers against the Plaintiff, Ima Victim.

5. Furthermore, the Defendants acted deliberately with knowledge of a high degree of probability of harm and reckless indifference to the consequences to the Plaintiff, Ima Victim.

6. The conduct of XYZ Law Firm and Malpractice Lawyer, jointly, severally, and in the alternative, constituted gross negligence.

7. As a direct and proximate result of the Defendants wanton, reckless, malicious, willful conduct, and gross negligence, the Plaintiff has suffered damages.

WHEREFORE, Plaintiff, Mr. Ima Victim demands judgment against XYZ Law Firm and Mr. Malpractice Lawyer, jointly, severally, and in the alternative, for:

A. Compensatory Damages;
B. Punitive Damages;
C. Interest;
D. Costs of suit;
E. Attorneys fees;
F. Damages for Emotional Distress and Mental Anguish;
G. Special and Consequential Damages; and
H. Any other relief the Court may deem equitable and just.

ELEVENTH COUNT

1. Plaintiff, Ima Victim, repeats and reiterates each and every paragraph of the First, Second, Third, Fourth, Fifth, Sixth, Seventh, Eighth, Ninth, and Tenth Counts of the Complaint as though the same were set forth at length herein.

2. The Defendants, Malpractice Lawyer and XYZ Law Firm, misrepresented, concealed, and otherwise made statements to Ima Victim which they knew to be false or should have known were false.

3. The Plaintiff, Ima Victim, relied upon those statements to his detriment.

4. As a direct and proximate result of the concealment, fraud, and misrepresentation, both intentional and negligent, by the Defendants, XYZ Law Firm and Malpractice Lawyer, the Plaintiff, Ima Victim, was caused to suffer damages, including special damages.

5. [Recite specific dates and facts surrounding the allegations of fraud, misrepresentation and concealment.]

WHEREFORE, Plaintiff, Ima Victim, demands judgment against XYZ Law Firm and Malpractice Lawyer, severally, jointly, and in the alternative, for:

A. Compensatory Damages;
B. Punitive Damages;
C. Interest;
D. Costs of suit;
E. Attorneys fees;
F. Special Damages; and
G. Any other relief the Court may deem equitable and just.

_____
Good Guy
Attorney for Plaintiff

JURY DEMAND

The Plaintiff demands a trial by jury on all issues.

_____
Good Guy
Attorney for Plaintiff

CERTIFICATION

It is hereby certified that this matter is not the subject of any other action pending in any Court or pending arbitration proceeding, and that no other action or arbitration proceedings is contemplated.

_____

Good Guy
Attorney for Plaintiff

SAMPLE SUMMONS [FIRST FORM SUMMONS] FOR NEW JERSEY RESIDENTS

Good Guy, Esq.
123 Justice Lane
Anywhere, New Jersey 00000
(201) 123-4567
Attorney for Plaintiff

SUPERIOR COURT OF NEW JERSEY
LAW DIVISION — MORRIS COUNTY
DOCKET NO. A-1234-89

Ima Victim
                    Plaintiff
                         vs.
Malpractice Lawyer and
XYZ Law Firm, Jointly, Severally,
and in the Alternative
                    Defendants
	Civil Action
	
	SUMMONS

The State of New Jersey, to the Above Named Defendant(s):

YOU ARE HEREBY SUMMONED in a Civil Action in the Superior Court of New Jersey, instituted by the above named plaintiff(s), and required to serve upon the attorney(s) for the plaintiff(s), whose name and office address appears above, an answer to the annexed complaint within 20 days after the service of the summons and complaint upon you, exclusive of the day of service. If you fail to answer, judgment by default may be rendered against you for the relief demanded in the complaint. You shall promptly file your answer and proof of service thereof in duplicate* with the Clerk of the Superior Court at _____*, in accordance with the rules of civil practice and procedure.

If you cannot afford to pay an attorney, call a Legal Services Office. An individual not eligible for free legal assistance may obtain a referral

to an attorney by calling a county lawyer referral service. These numbers may be listed in the yellow pages of your phone book or may be obtained by calling the New Jersey State Bar Association Lawyer Referral Service tollfree 800-852-0127 (within New Jersey) or 201-249-5000 (from out of state). The phone numbers for the county in which this action is pending are: Lawyer Referral Service,   ,
Legal Services Office

Dated: , 19   _____

Clerk of the Superior Court

Name of defendant to be served: Malpractice Lawyer and XYZ Law Firm

Address for service:
    C/O XYZ Law Firm
    Get Rich Quick Rd.
    Morristown, NJ

*For direct filing, add address for County Clerk and strike "in duplicate."

For Trenton filing add CN-971, Trenton, N.J. 08625.

31-N.J. Summons-Superior Court	Copyright 1980 by
(Revised Feb. 1988)	All-State Legal Supply Co.
	One Commerce Drive
	Cranford, NJ 07016

RVST - 2

SAMPLE LETTER TO SECURE THE RETURN OF THE FILE

February 17, 1989

Malpractice Lawyer
XYZ Law Firm
Get Rich Quick Road
Morristown, NJ 00000

    Re: Ima Victim

Dear Mr. Malpractice Lawyer and XYZ Law Firm:

Please be advised that I demand the return of my entire file. In the alternative, I demand a photocopy of my entire file.

I trust this letter will meet with your immediate attention.

Very truly yours,

Ima Victim
1 Poor House Road
Morristown, NJ 00000
(201)122-3456

SAMPLE ATTORNEY'S LETTER TO SECURE FILE

February 17, 1989

Malpractice Lawyer
XYZ Law Firm
Get Rich Quick Road
Morristown, New Jersey 00000

    Re: Ima Victim

Dear Mr. Malpractice Lawyer and XYZ Law Firm:

Please be advised this office represents Mr. Ima Victim, whom you formally represented in connection with Mr. Victim's accident of January 1, 1985. Kindly be further advised I am providing to you herewith an Authorization for the release of Mr. Victim's entire file to me.

Kindly advise me what arrangements need to be made in order for you to either release the file or provide me with a photocopy of Mr. Victim's file.

I trust this letter will meet with your immediate attention.

Very truly yours,

Good Guy, Esq.

AUTHORIZATION

I hereby authorize Good Guy, Esq. to receive the original or a photocopy of all files pertaining to any transactions in which I was a client.

DATED: ————————————   ————————————————
                                                Ima Victim

SAMPLE RESERVATION OF RIGHTS LETTER

February 17, 1989

Malpractice Lawyer
XYZ Law Firm
Get Rich Quick Road
Morristown, NJ 00000

Re: Insured: Malpractice Lawyer and XYZ Law Firm
Claimant: Ima Victim
File No.: 1234
Policy No.: 0001

Dear Mr. Malpractice Lawyer and XYZ Law Firm:

This will acknowledge receipt of your Summons and Complaint, wherein Mr. Malpractice Lawyer and XYZ Law Firm were sued by Mr. Ima Victim arising out of litigation from County of Morris, City of Morristown, New Jersey.

Please be advised that a file has been established under your policy no. of 0001 which has effective dates of 1/1/88 to 1/1/89 and provides limits of liability in the amount of $1,000,000.00 per claim and $1,000,000.00 in the aggregate with a deductible of $5,000.00 which applies to both indemnity and expense payments relative to this matter.

A review of the Complaint reveals that Mr. Malpractice Lawyer and the XYZ Law Firm are sued for both negligence and for a variety of other causes of action, many which are not covered under the terms and conditions of your policy of insurance. More specifically, your insurance policy excludes coverage for causes of action arising out of conduct such as fraud, duress, misrepresentation, and concealment. A further examination of the Complaint reveals that the Plaintiff, Mr. Ima Victim, is seeking punitive damages. The public policy of the State of New Jersey does not allow insurance companies to pay for punitive damages. The Complaint, moreover, seeks an unspecified amount of damages. Please be further advised that this Insurance Company will not be responsible nor will it pay any adverse settlement judgment or award which is in excess of the applicable policy limits.

[Recite relevant portions of the insurance policy for reference]

You may, if you so desire, at your own expense, retain private counsel of your choosing to represent your interests in connection with all non-covered grounds alleged in this Complaint. In the interim, in order that your interests may be protected at this time, we have assigned your defense to the law office of No Pay Defense Firm. You must cooperate with the representation in connection with the defense of this litigation. I would appreciate your affixing your signature at the bottom of this page evidencing your agreement with the assignment of No Pay Defense Firm to handle this case. If you should object to the assignment of No Pay Defense Firm, I would appreciate your advising me immediately upon receipt of this letter.

If you have any questions concerning this matter, please do not hesitate to contact me.

Very truly yours,

Professional Liability Claims Examiner
No Pay Insurance Company
We Don't Pay Road
No Deal, NJ 00000

I hereby consent to the defense of this lawsuit being assigned to No Pay Defense Firm and I consent to the defense of this lawsuit being handled under this Reservation of Rights.

_____   _____
Malpractice Lawyer   XYZ Law Firm

SAMPLE NON-WAIVER AGREEMENT

Agreement made by and between No Pay Insurance Company (hereinafter referred to as Insurance Company) and its insured, Malpractice Lawyer and XYZ Law Firm (hereinafter referred to as Insured), as follows:

RECITALS:

1. WHEREAS Insurance Company has issued a legal malpractice insurance policy to its insured under policy no. 0001, providing for coverage for a period of January 1, 1988 to January 1, 1989.

2. WHEREAS The Insured Law Firm was sued by Ima Victim for legal malpractice in a lawsuit arising out of the Superior Court of New Jersey under Complaint Docket No. A-1234-89 seeking damages from Insured Malpractice Lawyer and XYZ Law Firm.

3. WHEREAS The Insured has tendered the Complaint to the Insurance Company, claiming that there is coverage under the terms and conditions of the policy.

4. WHEREAS No Pay Insurance Company is contending that the defense of this claim should be made under reservation of rights, and it appearing that the interests of the Insured and the Insurance Company would be better served by the Insurance Company, assuming the defense of the claim.

NOW THEREFORE IT IS STIPULATED AND AGREED AS FOLLOWS:

1. It is understood and agreed that the Insurance Company shall proceed to investigate the facts of this claim during the defense of this lawsuit and, if it so chooses, to negotiate a settlement without prejudice to or without waiver of its rights with regard to Malpractice Lawyer and XYZ Law Firm on any coverage issues.

2. It is understood and agreed that the Insurance Company, by continuing with the defense of this claim, does not waive or invalidate any of the conditions of the policy in question and does not waive any rights whatsoever that it may have under the terms and conditions of the policy.

3. It is understood and agreed that the Insured by allowing the Insurance Company to provide a defense of this claim, does not waive or invalidate any of the conditions of the policy and does not waive or invalidate any rights whatsoever that it may have under the terms and conditions of the policy.

4. It is understood and agreed that the Insurance Company, without waiving any of its rights, may at its option at any time institute a Declaratory Judgment action to secure a judicial determination of the respective rights of the parties under the policy.

5. It is understood and agreed that the Insured without waiving any of its rights may at its option at any time institute a Declaratory Judgment action to secure a judicial determination of the respective rights of the parties under the policy.

6. The Insurance Company specifically reserves any and all rights it has under the policy in question to withdraw from the defense and/or to deny coverage for part, if not all, of any judgment, settlement, or award rendered against any Insured in connection with this matter.

7. The Insured specifically reserves any and all rights that it has under the policy to claim for costs of defense and/or indemnity for any judgment, settlement, or award rendered against it or any additional Insureds in connection with this matter.

8. No representations have been made by either the Insurance Company or the Insured to induce the other to execute this Agreement except as otherwise contained herein. It is mutually understood and agreed that neither the Insured nor the Insurance Company, by signing this agreement, shall be deemed to have waived or surrendered any of their respective rights and benefits under the terms and conditions of the policy in question.

All parties affirm that they have read this Agreement, have had the advice of counsel, and fully understand the terms and conditions hereof.

WHEREFORE, this ____ day of, 19____, the parties to this agreement have hereunto fixed their hand and seals and the corporate parties have caused this instrument to be duly executed by their authorized officers, intending to be legally bound.

_____

Malpractice Lawyer

_____   _____

No Pay Insurance Company   XYZ Law Firm

SAMPLE CONSENT FORM FOR
SETTLEMENT WITH ATTORNEY

Date: February 20, 1989

No Pay Insurance Company
We Don't Pay Road
No Deal, New Jersey 00000

Attn: Professional Liability Claim Examiner

Re: Insured: Malpractice Lawyer & XYZ Law Firm
      Claimant: Ima Victim
      File No.: 1234
      Policy No.: 0001

Dear Mr. Professional Liability Claim Examiner:

I do hereby give my written consent for the settlement of the above-
captioned matter. [This consent does not imply negligence or liability
on the attorney's part.]

Very truly yours,

_____

Malpractice Lawyer

_____

XYZ Law Firm
